Sell Your Music!

How to Profitably Sell Your Own Recordings Online

Mark W. Curran

NMD Books
Simi Valley, CA

NMD Books
Simi Valley, CA

© 2001 Mark W.Curran

Visit our Web site at http://www.NMDBooks.com.

Library of Congress Cataloging-in-Publication Data

Curran, Mark W.
    Sell Your Music: How to Profitably Sell Your Own Recordings Online / Mark W.Curran

p.   cm.
Includes bibliographical references and index.

ISBN: 0-9706773-5-9 (Softcover)

    1. Music—Marketing. 2. Marketing—Music.
          3. Internet—Marketing. 4. Business—Direct Distribution.
          5. Music—Publishing. 6. Publishing—Self-publishing. I. Title.

                2001 130284

Book Design by Virginia Lawrence, http://www.CogniText.com.

Cover Art by Robert Aulicino, http://www.AulicinoDesign.com.

First Edition March 2001

Preface

At the time of this writing, enormous changes have taken place in the music industry. For the first time in history since the inception of the pop music phenomenon in the late 1950's, musicians now have more opportunities to market their music directly to the consumer than ever before. The Internet has made the impossible possible. Using the power of the Internet, musicians can break the stranglehold the major record companies and their distribution arms have had on the record industry since the 1960's.

This book was prompted by my discovery that very little had been written about specific strategies and methods of direct marketing independent music through the Internet. Given the growth of such direct music marketing sites as MP3.com and the amazing popularity of the MP3 format among the general Web population, it was obvious that the time had come for such a book.

Thus began a long period of research and practical application.

Success in the creative arts has always boiled down to the economics of distribution. The cost of distribution forces the distribution entity to become highly selective when choosing artists to fill the pipeline.

This has left over 99% of the artists creating product without a proper distribution channel. Sadly, much of the world's greatest music has been left unheard.

Then the Internet arrived, and technology supplied a new distribution channel.

It is now possible for the independent musician to take control of his own destiny, to distribute his own product.

Now it is possible to produce master quality demos in the home, and market them directly to the consumer, for next to no cost. This simple fact has one of the largest industries in the world up in arms, and has created shock waves in every aspect of the music business.

This is as it should be, because innovations in popular music have always shaken up the status quo.

This book discusses the techniques I have used in marketing my own music directly to consumers. The book also outlines the experiences of others who have successfully marketed music online.

The essential information is here for you. Take advantage of this information, but I must issue one simple but essential caveat:

> None of the marketing methods described in this book will work unless they are applied, and applied on a consistent basis. If online music marketing is treated and worked like a business by the independent musician, these methods will serve as building blocks to a satisfying and profitable career as a self-employed musician.

But all things of value come at a cost.

It takes a great deal of time and hard work to make any business work, and direct distribution over the Internet is no exception. Give up the idea of instant wealth and easy money now, and you will not be disappointed later.

The bottom line is that it takes motivation, sweat, hard work, persistence, and a certain measure of luck to make it in the music business. The competition is staggering. The odds against great success are overwhelming.

The independent musician must have a well-defined marketing plan, and he must apply the plan daily. Armed with the proper tools, you will be well equipped in your journey of spreading your music to the world.

Use this book as a tool kit, a weapon in your arsenal to achieve your musical dreams. Experiment with the methods in this book and test your own methods.

If the task appears overwhelming to you, remember that the journey of a thousand miles begins with one small step.

Nobody can market your music like you can, because nobody else cares as much about it, and nobody else will take the time and care to do it like you can. Unless you are wealthy, resist the temptation to hire others to do the job you can do yourself, at least at the beginning.

That advice may sound crazy coming from a consultant who makes his living doing the job for others, but it is a truth I make clear to all of my clients. Learn how to do it yourself, then you will be in a position to hire others to do it for you.

Here's the potential: the Internet makes it possible to sell your music to millions of people all over the world. This book gives you methods and strategies you can use to achieve that potential.

Mark W. Curran

January 2001

The Music Marketing Company
http://www.musicmarketingco.com
Los Angeles, California

Foreword

Digital technology changes quickly, and in the Internet business, digital technology morphs with amazing speed. In this book, I will refer to MP3 as the compression method currently most popular in use on the net, but inevitably, MP3 will be replaced by MP4, or some other technology. Thus, when you see the term "MP3", you should automatically replace that term with the latest, greatest compression format.

Although you may be reading this book many months or years beyond its publication date, be assured that the publication date does not make this book any less powerful. Rather, the principles explained here are universal. The concepts and methods contained within these covers are, and will continue to be, invaluable tools no matter where the technology takes us.

The methods discussed in this book are based on age-old marketing principles, but applied to today's new technology. This book enables independent musicians to exploit their music and become virtual direct retailers on a global scale that was never before possible.

The fortunes that can be made using these techniques are boundless. The unlimited potential for the expansion of the digital horizon is limited only by our imaginations, for the future we imagine today will become tomorrow's reality.

This book is for those with the courage to dream big and make their own imagined future happen, not by dreams alone, but by the application of creative energy, tangible marketing principles and hard work.

This book is for those who know that it's time to establish their own piece of the American Dream on a global scale, to reach the masses with their own songs, their own records, their own music.

Acknowledgements

I would like to thank the following people for all their help in preparing this book. My editor, Virginia Lawrence of CogniText, for her patience and her dedication, Robert Aulicino for his great cover design, Dan Poynter for showing me the way, Faith Rivera, Ernest Cortazar Jr. and Sr, and all the industry experts and groups who consented for an interview for this book.

Also to Nancy Nicolas for all her love and support, and my little munchkins, Aimee and Alan for demonstrating the wonders of childhood.

I must also give praise and thanks to my late father, William F. Curran, for being such a supportive and loving Dad, and to my mother, Dorothy, for her wisdom and understanding.

For Dave Love, Tom Haney, Dary Cauller and all my buds back in Pennsylvania, without all of you this book would not have been possible, for all of you have contributed to this book in your own special way.

Table of Contents

Appendix 4

Appendix 5

Appendix 6

Appendix 7

Appendix 8

1
Direct Music Distribution and the New Digital Revolution

The implications of the new digital music revolution are staggering. Thousands of musicians and recording artists have bypassed the major record companies and their distribution arms to go direct, marketing their music in a variety of ways to the general public.

The Internet is one of the most powerful tools for accomplishing direct distribution. The Internet reaches literally millions of people for next to no direct dollar cost.

Some of the success stories of artists who have used the Web successfully are featured in sidebars throughout this book. Their stories should act as motivators, and their accomplishments are merely a foreshadow of things to come.

Direct distribution of self-generated product will become the dominating market force of the 21st century in all areas of the arts. The Internet will be the dominant medium for achieving this direct distribution. The day has come when musicians, filmmakers, authors, and artists of all kinds can place their creations online and allow the public to buy them directly.

The advantages to both consumer and artist are manifold. The ability to sample the product online before buying, the advantage of purchasing the product at a price lower than usual, and the relative ease of ordering are just a few of the benefits to the consumer.

The artist benefits from being able to reach his target market directly at minimal cost, without having to go through a middleman/distributor. The artist can also move quickly on trends and nuances in the marketplace. Such immediate responses to the marketplace would not be possible using conventional distribution methods, because of their extended turnaround times.

The digital revolution is changing the world at an astounding rate. Direct distribution is one of the economic miracles that have occurred as a result of the digital revolution. Direct distribution allows the independent musician the power to niche market their product worldwide.

This book shows different methods and strategies to be used in direct distribution. You will also read the success stories of musicians who have accomplished their wildest dreams by marketing their music online.

Overview of the Market

Current statistics show that in 2000, there were at least 34 million online music sales. These are only the reported figures from RIAA, and do not take into account the thousands of indie labels sprouting up worldwide.

> **RIAA**
> Recording Industry
> Association of America

> **Indie**
> Independent, as in indie label or indie musician

Projections on the sales of music online are expected to reach 1.7 billion dollars in 2001, and may even exceed that number by the publication date of this book. These projected sales are only the tip of the iceberg, for they do not include the sales of the independents in distributing their own product. The market is expected to grow exponentially as more people go online, and they are going online at a rate of about 1.5 million new users per week.

Considering that many of these new users meet the demographic model of the consumer most expected to purchase music online, projections for sales by the independent musician are limitless.

Now that consumers have the ability to preview music clips and purchase them immediately with their credit cards, consumers can make the impulse music buy directly, from the comfort of their own homes. We know that the public embraces the shop at home economic model. We see the huge success of home shopping networks on cable television, as well as the phenomenal growth of such online distribution systems as Amazon, CD-Now, and Barnes and Noble.

Price is another factor which has played into the hands of the indie musician. With the average price of CDs hitting upwards of $18 - $20, consumers are realizing that purchasing product from local retail outlets is not cost effective.

The tools for reaching your potential audience are at your fingertips. It's up to you to adopt an effective marketing strategy and carry it through. As Microsoft says, "Where do you want to go today?"

To quote the Beatles, "To the toppermost of the poppermost!"

The Power of the Impulse Buy

Never underestimate the power of the impulse buy. The impulse buy drives retail sales, and it is the lifeblood of Internet sales. Once a consumer has sampled your music and wants to buy it, the consumer carries out only a few keystrokes, and your product can be on its way to him in seconds.

The beauty of marketing your music on the Internet is that we can now instantly deliver an optimal quality digital download of the product to the consumer. The download can be completed before the physical product would be packed for shipping and physical delivery. This is impulse buying at its best, and this speed and simplicity explains the success of such music sales sites as MP3.com.

Remember, it is your job to capture the imagination of the consumer, inform him of your product, deliver a quality demonstration of that product, and capture the sale.

Is Your Product Good Enough?

This question is a loaded one. Since "good" and bad" are always determined by the buyer, you can make a pretty fair assumption that your music will be marketable to some segment of the music buying public. The degree of penetration in any target market is difficult to determine until you undertake your marketing and sales program.

My own criteria for determining quality, although still subjective, are:

Is the quality of the recorded music as high as possible, with no distortion, noise, or other unwanted artifacts?

Are the vocals on pitch?

Are the songs interesting?

Is the product packaging attractive?

We know that the question of quality with regard to musical performance is a very subjective thing. Our current industry shows there is a market for just about anything, from *avant garde* to the most mundane, and a quick sampling of what is selling in stores and online today is a good indication of that fact.

For example, the Grateful Dead are arguably the best or worst band in rock history, depending on your taste. Their sales indicate their fan base will buy anything they record. They are also masters at independent promotion, and have been selling their own music and merchandise for over four decades without the help of any major record company.

I don't like the Grateful Dead, never have, never will. But there are hundreds of thousands of "deadheads" out there who do, and that's what matters.

The Grateful Dead have learned to work their market, and although they are not for everyone, they have prospered very well.

There are major artists out there now who defy my criteria for quality, yet continue selling their music. Can Kris Kristopherson sing on pitch? No. Does he sell albums? You bet. He's a great songwriter, and his off-pitch voice adds an interesting dimension to his lyrics.

Even a terrible voice can sell. Look at Tom Waits. This guy has a persona right out of a Dashiell Hammett novel, and his approach and songwriting are unique. Tom Waits' gravelly rasp delivers his catchy melodies and unusual lyrics in a way that appeals to a small audience. How small? Small enough to make him a millionaire!

Fact is, there are recording artists all over our airwaves that have arguably questionable talent. But the lesson is in understanding that talent is subjective, and has little to do with marketability or sales.

The point here is that you don't have to appeal to as wide an audience as possible when marketing your music online. Whatever you have to offer, there are people out there who will buy it.

Think of a major selling group you dislike, and you will see this principle in action.

Try not to worry about commercial potential or your music's projected level of acceptance. You cannot know these things in advance, so why let it impede the joy of creativity?

Make your music with passion, make the packaging attractive, offer value for the money, and push it hard. These are the tenets of great online marketing.

If you do it and you do it well, you will find an audience for your product.

Music Myths Exposed

First let's examine some of the common misconceptions about making it in the music business.

The common view is that if you are a really great singer, musician or songwriter, or that you are in a really great band, your talent will eventually be recognized by a talent scout or record company executive, or some similar such person.

As a result of this, the belief goes, you will be signed to a record deal, and whisked into a recording studio. In the studio you will record a record that will be released, played on radio stations worldwide, sold by the millions in stores, and you will go on a giant concert tour and make millions.

The sad reality is, this rarely happens.

Often times, the very best talent gets passed over for a group or artist that happens to know someone inside the business. The music industry is very much an "insider" industry. Contacts and personal relationships are often the key to the golden door.

But once inside that door, the magic doesn't begin.

If you or your group are signed to a record company deal, and you go into the recording studio, you will be charged against your advance and your royalties for all expenses incurred during the recording process, and the resulting tour.

The record company has to hire song pluggers that go out to the radio stations promoting newly breaking albums and singles. If, against all odds, your music gets played and sells in the stores (a very big if), then you get to tour and pay back the record company all the money they loaned you to get your career started.

When it comes to making money from your record sales, the reality is that you will make a very small percentage of your sales. For every copy sold, you will get a standard royalty, but expenses will be deducted from that royalty.

Record companies have some very creative accountants who can keep you in the red for years, an indentured servant to the very system you tried so hard to join.

The record business has worked this way for years, and this is why many major artists are in debt to their record company, touring forever and making nothing. It's no wonder stars become addicts, trash hotel rooms and jump off buildings. It's enough to drive a person insane.

But now, you have the choice, as many artists have done, to go the distance yourself. To create and sell your own product. To do it your way, to build your own audience, and to reap the rewards yourself.

2
Creating the Product

There are several ways to go about selling your music online.

The first and easiest way is to create songs, convert them to a digital format, (currently the most functional and popular is MP3) and market them as a collection of songs on your Web site. You can call your collection of songs a "CD," even though your music consists of individual songs and are not contained on CD format.

The best way to market songs in this fashion is to sell them from your own Web site, while also listing your music on the many online music portal services.

MP3.com

The best known, and most effective of these portals is the granddaddy of them all, MP3.com.

MP3.com Web site - The Granddaddy of Indie Promo

While most musicians who know online music will know all about MP3.com, here is a quick rundown of what they do:

- They allow you to upload samples of your music to your own customizable Web page, and will help you market your songs to their huge database of members.

- Act as partners with you in selling your music, even creating CDs that can be sold as hard products, and will even ship them for you, for 50% of the sale.

- Will pay you for each download request your music generates.

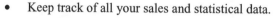

- Keep track of all your sales and statistical data.

- Implement marketing and sales programs to help drive people to your page.

MP3.com is essential to the online musician, as it is the biggest indie music portal on the Web. They generate hundreds of thousands of dollars in revenue for their music partners, each and every month. MP3.com is also an indispensable resource to find other musicians in your area and around the world for discussion and collaboration.

This book features many successful artists who have used MP3.com and earned fortune and fame, simply by listing their music at the portal. They will reveal their techniques and experiences and give insight into their own unique approaches.

There are, and will continue to be, many other portals similar to MP3.com, and the smart indie will do well to research them and use them all. The more portals where you actually list your site, the better.

Audio Formats and their Uses

As Web and digital technology continue to evolve, so do the audio formats for delivering your music to the masses. At present, MP3 is the most accepted format. New formats will emerge, most likely leaving MP3 in the dust. A new MP4 format is in the making, as well as several others with similar compression schemes.

Without getting into the technical aspects of what these audio formats do and how they differ, from a marketing perspective it is enough for the musician to know that these formats compress or squeeze your music into packets that can be transmitted easily over the Internet.

> **Common File Formats on the Internet**
>
> The most common audio file formats found on the Internet are µ-law (.au), AIFF, WAVE (.wav),
>
> Macintosh sound resources (snd), and QuickTime movies (.mov). The single greatest reason for their popularity is cross-platform compatibility and use.
>
> Other formats, notably MOD and AIFC files, have attractive characteristics, but have not been widely accepted on UNIX, IBM-PC compatible, and Macintosh platforms. Conversely, newer formats, such as MPEG-compressed audio and video, may become common on the Internet due solely to the comparatively substantial benefits they yield. (source: Vince Lombardi)

The two essential differences in playback functionality are:

1. Streaming Media

   Streaming media, most popularly known as Real Audio, allows the surfer to hear the music live without having to download any files to their computer.

2. Downloadable Media

Downloadable media are music files that must be downloaded or saved to the hard drive first, then played. The advantage to the downloadable media is that the song file can be saved and listened to later, burned to a CD, or even delivered to one of the many new playback and storage systems now emerging on the market.

It is important to realize that the formats will likely change frequently, and as they do, higher levels of quality and smaller file sizes will be achieved. Don't get hung up on the technology side of things unless you want to impede your progress as an aggressive marketer.

The recording industry makes its money on changing formats; keep your eye on the creation of the product and leave the bits and bytes to the engineers. What they will be able to achieve in the coming years will astound, amaze and delight, and will always keep consumers reaching for their credit cards.

For the musician just starting out in the digital formatting of music for distribution over the Internet, the process goes something like this:

1. Create your music
2. Mixdown to analog or digital medium
3. Convert analog or digital file to a .WAV file
4. Convert the .WAV file to an .MP3 file

> **Mixdown**
> Mixing a multi-track recording down to stereo

This somewhat cumbersome procedure will probably evolve to a simpler process. Soon we will be making the MP3 file without the intermediary .WAV file, and later we can expect to make the MP3 file while making or mixing the analog or digital master.

The above conversion process is a relatively simple one, and can be accomplished by the use of several shareware or freeware programs easily downloaded from the Web.

As newer formats, machines and processes are perfected, there will be faster and more efficient ways to make your music Internet-ready.

The programs I use are:

- Cool Edit 2000 — http://www.cooledit.com/

Will record your audio through a standard sound card in stereo.

Recording on your hard drive with CoolEdit2000

- MusicMatch Jukebox — http://www.musicmatch.com/

   Converts .WAV files to MP3 files compatible with most online portal services. This is the official software for MP3.com.

A popular MP3 Player and Wave File Converter

There are other software packages that do pretty much the same things that these programs do. However, the programs are all essentially the same.

You'll find that it takes a little trial and error to get decent quality recordings as you make your digital music and convert your files. I am not a computer wizard, and I found myself getting a bit frustrated when I first started converting my analog files to digital, and then making MP3 files from the digital files.

But after I made the conversion several times, I discovered how easy the process really is. I also discovered how amazing the quality can be when you do it right.

Digital can play little tricks on your ears when you are mixing. You may find that your vocals or other instruments can get "buried" in the mix. That's why it's important to play back the MP3 file on a larger stereo system's speakers to hear if there are any anomalies in the recording playback.

Mixing for digital is much the same as mixing for analog, but you should be aware that certain phase and frequency shifts can occur. Those shifts can cause certain instruments and vocals to vary in volume, tone, and attack.

When I am recording my own music with vocals, I always mix my lead vocal as far to the front as possible, making it much louder than the instruments. This is a standard procedure for me in normal analog mixing, but in digital mixing for the Internet, it is especially critical. There is nothing worse than not being able to hear the singer, or to not understand the words.

Keep the vocals strong and prominent, allowing an extra bit more volume than you would normally.

A Word about Length

It's a good idea to keep your song lengths at around 3 1/2 minutes. This is the standard length for commercial radio airplay, and is their accepted norm for commercial pop tunes. Not that you must adhere to commercial pop radio formats, but it cuts down on the file sizes, and keeps the listener interested in the song.

If you are recording dance music without lyrics, such as trance, house, or acid, or music containing lots of dance loops, record two versions; a 12 minute dance mix, and then a shorter 3-4 minute radio edit.

You can place your extended mix version on your CD, and keep the shorter version for the version that can stream from your site. The edited version is also the ideal size for posting on MP3.com.

The beauty of indie recording is that you can record your songs to any length you want. But remember to always record a version with an Internet friendly file size.

In a few years, the majority of surfers will be on broadband connections, but for now, 56k appears to be the norm. Make sure to accommodate the slower connections by keeping file sizes user-friendly and manageable.

Defining your Target Market

To achieve the best results from your marketing efforts, defining your target market is key. Since those who purchase music online have a wide variety of tastes, it is hard to be "all things to all people." If you wish to sell successfully on the Web, you must determine what style of music your creations fall under, and then find the market that wants that style.

Now, this can run counter to the indie spirit of recording hybrids and fusions of styles, in much the same way as commercial radio and conventional record companies "pigeonhole" music to reach their target audience, but it doesn't mean the death knell of creativity.

While it is somewhat harder to market fusions, such as jazz-rock, country-reggae, hip-hop-folk, etc., (and there are endless combinations) it is not impossible. It just specializes your niche further.

This can be both a blessing and disguise. While your market narrows, your niche becomes more focused, and the more focused your niche becomes, the easier it is to reach the people in your niche.

One Way to Approach the Problem of Specialized Niches:

Let's say you have a style of music that could best be classified as jazz-rock, with a touch of Pop. Find a popular group that is as close to your style as possible.

In this case, for the sake of example, if you determine your style is closest to that of the popular fusion group Steely Dan, then you can seek out fan clubs, discussion groups, bulletin boards, mailing lists and fan sites of Steely Dan.

Since you know the people that visit these areas are Steely Dan fanatics, you've established your target market, in this case, a niche-specialized market, of jazz-rock fusion fans.

From there, you can market directly to this group by any number of methods as will be described to you in the upcoming section on "marketing."

The point is that you have located a group of people who are likely to be receptive to your music. If they enjoy the jazz-rock-pop fusion of Steely

Dan, they are sales prospects for listening to, and hopefully buying, your music.

If your musical style runs to a more standard category, such as country, your prospective fan base is much larger. The larger or broader the fan base, the more places to market your music to that fan base.

But the catch is, not all country fans are going to like your music. Country has many sub-genres and styles. Some people like Garth Brooks. Some like female vocalists like Leeanne Rimes, while others prefer a more traditional country, like Lorrie Morgan.

Some people's taste run to male vocal new traditionalists, like Randy Travis or Dwight Yoakum, or the older country-western traditionalists like George Jones and Johnny Cash, or even the "bridge" country artists like Merle Haggard.

Since there are so many variations on a given genre, it is important to be able to determine what sub-genre your music falls under, locate a similar artist, and then go after that niche group.

Now, I can almost hear the scowls coming from indie artists who feel that their music should stand on its own merit without being placed into any category, the very attribute that made these pop artists stand out from the crowd.

But while you are building an audience, it is important to realize that your music is a product, and in order to sell that product effectively, you must have some way of determining who your target market is.

If your music contains too many diverse elements, it will have a difficult time finding a fan base. Which is not a reason to abandon your style, just realize that if your style is too *avant-garde* to at least appeal to a popular genre or sub-genre, your audience may be more difficult to build.

Importance of Demographics

Marketing professionals work with a method called "demographics" as a tool to define and serve certain age groups and interests.

We define demographics as: the statistical characteristics of human populations (such as age or income) used especially to identify markets.

To apply the demographic methodology to music, you should first determine whether you have a style of music that appeals to a certain age group. If so, you can locate the common interests of that age group, and you can market your products in places where the music will be seen by that age group.

For example, fans of the popular group Backstreet Boys may share the common demographic of having an interest in roller blading.

By frequenting the same places as roller blading enthusiasts, you would have a good chance of reaching your target audience for your music, provided that your music was similar to that of the Backstreet Boys.

This opens up an infinite number of possibilities for reaching your demographic audience. What about advertising your CD in an online newsletter that is dedicated to roller blading? You might even take this idea a step further, and create your own advertising venue by starting your own roller blading newsletter incorporating your ad top and bottom.

Another variation on this theme might be to put up your own Web site catering to roller blading. You can have your music playing as embedded audio files every time someone comes to your roller blading homepage.

Be forewarned that these ideas can spin into time-eating monsters if you aren't careful. These ideas do serve to demonstrate that there are many ways to market to your target audience, and demographics are just one tool to help you achieve this.

Inverse Marketing Strategies

Inverse marketing is another such tool. This method involves establishing your target market first, then creating the product to fit.

Granted, this is a more business-like approach to creativity. This method is not for everyone, but it does work.

To use Backstreet Boys example as a reference, you might decide to use inverse marketing and research your market prior to deciding what kind of music you want to sell.

This works best for musicians who are adept at creating many different styles of music, and may have no particular preference as to which direction to take.

To use myself as an example, I noticed on MP3.com that there were a great many country music artists that were not selling very much product. Despite the popularity of country music worldwide, I noticed that surfers who frequent this portal tend to like a dance-style sub-genre called trance.

Judging by the frequency of downloads of songs and groups serving this market, I concluded that if I were to create good trance music, I would have a ready market. I listened to many of the more popular downloads, and began to form my inverse marketing strategy.

Since I have a small home recording studio, I was able to jump on this trend, and record some very catchy and innovative trance cuts, even though I had little experience or knowledge of the genre. The fact that I also really liked this style of music was helpful in the creative process.

Consequently, I released a CD entitled "Trance Dreams," which has enjoyed great popularity and brisk sales.

Inverse marketing is not for everyone, though, and I would discourage anyone from recording music they do not enjoy creating. But if you enjoy many different styles of music, and have the ability to create on demand, inverse marketing is a great strategy for jump starting your online marketing business.

Importance of Recording Quality

As we mentioned earlier, certain aspects of quality are subjective. When I say quality, I mean that you must make sure that you make your recordings on the highest quality equipment you can afford. This means that your recordings should have no pops, noise, or other artifacts. In addition, that there should be as little tape hiss as possible.

If you are recording in the digital domain, tape hiss should not be a factor. If you are taking your music to the analog domain at any step in the process, tape hiss is your worst enemy.

I take painstaking steps to ensure that each instrument I record, including voice, is captured as cleanly as possible. That may seem an obvious statement, but I am amazed at the number of low quality recordings I hear online. Noisy and poorly mixed songs are the mark of an amateur, and surfers are more sophisticated than you may give them credit for.

Before someone parts with their hard-earned money for a recording, he is going to carefully evaluate your product. If that product is not comparable to the standard of professionally recorded product in your genre, you will lose the sale.

Take the time and care to do it right the first time. You will save time and money. Offering a quality product, you will make more sales than you would if you rushed the process and banged out a quick mix for the masses.

Consumers are sharp and they have a keen ear for quality. Shoot for the very best you can do. If your final product is high quality, that product will be appreciated by a larger audience.

Art vs. Commerce

It has often been said that art and commerce make strange bedfellows, which is just another way of saying that creativity and money are very often at odds with one another.

It's an endless argument. To what degree does an artist bend to the demands of the marketplace? At what point does he draw the line in the sand and say, "This is my limit, I am not going to cross the line to make more sales." We do know that all artists will eventually arrive at their commercial limit when creating their music.

Unfortunately, many artists create impossible double binds for themselves. They want to maintain their individuality and their unique sound. Yet if that unique sound does not find a ready market, the artists complain that they cannot make sales, and resign themselves to recording demos that never see the light of day.

These same artists seem resigned to martyrdom. They place their tapes in the bottom of a desk drawer, and stand defiantly and with great bitterness in the unemployment line.

Some artists work at jobs they can't stand. While working they dream of the day they will achieve stardom with their music. They expect that day to come when either the consumer or the music industry will recognize their music for the masterpiece it is.

Much of the time, this industry enlightenment never happens. In my view, this is a cop-out. If you are a musician, and you want to make money selling your music, then your job is to entertain people. Your job is to give people a product they appreciate as valuable, a product they are willing to buy.

If you want to play your own unique brand of music that is not selling, go ahead. Continue to record it and try to build an audience. At the same time, you may want to consider an alternate plan of action.

Remember the music business is a business, and must be treated as such. Creative people often drop the ball when it comes to business, and the business side is where many artists fall through the cracks.

The more successful artists often hire managers, attorneys and accountants to handle their money for them. Of course, the road is littered with the carcasses of successful recording artists who lost their fortunes to middlemen.

Then there are the recording artists whose music will never be heard by anyone, because their creators were too proud to serve their market.

Decide whether you want your music to be an occupation that makes you money, or a just a fun hobby. If you just want to play your own music and try to sell it, great. If you are happy when your music doesn't make you a dime, you are fine.

But if you want your music to be enjoyed by many people, and you want those people to buy it, you'd better be sure you are providing them with something they are willing to purchase. I am not suggesting that you "sell out," or that you record music you do not believe in. Rather, I suggest that you look at the realities of the marketplace. Evaluate your music closely to determine whether it can survive the rigors of the sales process.

My personal philosophy is that one should never do something solely for the money.

But doing something you enjoy and getting paid for it is the Holy Grail of our society. Don't fight yourself. Don't be your own worst enemy while trying to realize your dream of making money from your music.

The Inner Critic

While we are on this subject, it's important to mention one formidable opponent in your quest for artistic freedom. That opponent is yourself, your inner critic.

The inner critic can be an unfair and cruel taskmaster. The inner critic feeds you false information about the value of your product and your talent.

Often, we are our own worst critics. We evaluate our own work and conclude that it is not fit for dissemination. Then we destroy the work or lock it away forever. History is full of brilliant artists who drove themselves to madness by creating masterpieces and then destroying each piece because of self-doubt.

Now the inner critic can serve as an effective means of quality control. However, the inner critic must be reined in. You should remember that when you are judging your own work, you may be incorrectly judging that your work is inferior. The reality of the situation could be very well a different story.

Create openly and without judgment. Tap into the flow of creative energy we all draw upon as our life force, and suspend your judgments for a later time. Creativity cannot flow unimpeded while your inner critic is engaged in a constant process of critical evaluation. I believe that Jean Sibelius said it best, for both the inner and outer critic, when the wise hand wrote:

"Pay no attention to what the critics say; there has never been set up a statue in honor of a critic."

This advice extends to the times when you listen to others who criticize your work. Commonly harsh critics are exhibiting their own poor self-image. Wayne Dyer wrote, "Be not concerned with the good opinions of other people." The fact that your music finds a market and people are willing to pay good money for it is justification enough that you are doing something right.

I must also mention at this point that you may be writing and playing music to please only one person, and that is yourself. This is perfectly fine. In the end, we must all be happy with our creations and proud of them.

But if our work is to be accepted by others, the truest form of acceptance is not by critical acclaim. True acceptance is demonstrated by the people who are willing to purchase your music with their own hard-earned funds.

We are all plagued by self-critical and negative inner demons. Don't let these demons ruin your creative spirit, but let them impel you to greater heights.

When creating your music, let the process flow, get it down on paper or on tape, and reserve your judgment until later, when the creative urge has passed. If your work still seems inferior, ask for a professional opinion, and the views of others who can listen objectively.

The issue of criticism can be a dilemma. On one hand, you want objectivity. On the other hand, many people thrive on tearing apart the work of others, regardless of its merit.

Be sure to take criticism with a grain of salt. Do find the common points of several different critiques and re-evaluate your work in light of those points. If you believe the work could be improved based on a combination of outer and inner input, then do so.

In the final analysis, it is always best to follow your heart.

Product Length

In this business, the ideal product you will be creating is a collection of songs that run a TRT or total running time of 40 minutes or more. These songs can be sold as a single entity as a digital download, as a burned CD, as a cassette, or all three.

Give value for the money. I like to include about 45 minutes of music, or 11-12 songs that run about 3-4 minutes each. Instrumental or trance albums may have longer cuts, but you should include radio edits for each longer cut.

You will be placing your radio edits online as either Lo-Fi or Hi-Fi streaming or downloadable clips on your own Web site. You will also place the clips on music portal sites, such as MP3.Com.

You really must create a CD. Having a CD will enable you to also sell offline at your live performances, and to sell on consignment at record stores.

Although offline marketing is a different topic requiring its own book, keep the offline market in mind that when creating your product to sell online. Your product will lead a double life offline, and that offline marketing will boost your online efforts.

Be sure to place your Web site address (URL) on all of your packaging, business cards, letterheads, press releases, and CD covers. When every piece of marketing material carries your URL, you will drive traffic to your site to make more sales.

Product Price

Keep your online price points lower than retail to increase volume sales. The standard price for an independent CD being sold online is about $10-$15. If you price your CD too high, you will decrease your sales, while selling it too low will cut into your profit margin.

Your buyers have a keen sense for value. Give them the highest value at the lowest sensible price.

Packaging is Everything

When you have completed your CD, pay special attention to the artwork and layout of your graphics. Your package should look every bit as good as the products being released by the major labels.

Many people are impulse buyers. You'd be surprised at how many people will buy your CD for the cover alone. We are a visually stimulated society, and we love vivid colors and appealing images. Make sure to take advantage of this when packaging your CD.

Take your notes and ideas to your CD manufacturer. Many CD manufacturers offer inexpensive graphics and printing services which can turn your notes and ideas into a work of art. (You will find a list of CD manufacturers/packagers at the back of this book.)

The four-color printing process is more expensive than black and white, but I think it's well worth the money. Of course, there are innovative and spectacular ways to use black and white, and a good designer can work wonders with this less expensive option.

MP3.com allows you to design your own covers and artwork for your online CD, called Digital Audio Music (DAM). If you will be using their DAM service, MP3.com will print your artwork for you, so that you don't have to worry about the physical packaging.

I consider the DAM method as a great way to start if you are on a low budget. However, I expect that eventually you will want to package your own CDs to take into the offline world.

Leaving the packaging of your CD to others cuts into your profits, and leaves you with no real product to sell on your own.

When packaging your own CD, be sure to include on the back cover a list of songs, numbered in the order they appear on your CD, with the running time of each song. This back cover list helps programmers who are playing your music on offline and online radio stations. The programmers can use your list to compile and manage their schedule and playlists.

Importance of Text

While we are on the subject of the back cover, the wording on the back cover of your CD can also enhance your package, enticing the browser to buy. Good copy can work miracles, as can the magic of descriptive, "Kodak moment" lyrics.

For another nice touch, you can print your lyrics on the inside of your CD insert. Printing your lyrics makes sense and helps the listener fully experience your music. When selling online, make sure to include the full lyrics to your songs on your Web site.

When using MP3.Com and other portal sites, you are given an option to place the lyrics with your music, so the listener can follow along with the lyrics as he listens. Use this option every time.

An excellent book I recommend highly as essential reading covering all aspects of creating and selling your own music offline is: *The Musician's Guide to Making & Selling Your Own CDs & Cassettes* by Stanfield. This book is available at most bookstores or you can purchase it directly at my Web site.

Layout and Design Templates

Using design templates as a guide will make it easier to put your graphics together. These simple layout guides act as a map to the placement of text and images on your record jackets and inserts.

Diskmakers offers many such templates at:

http://www.discmakers.com/music/templates/

Manufacturing

Even if you are starting out just selling your music exclusively in digital form through downloads, at some point, you must have CDs made of your recordings. Physical CDs are essential for mail order sales, point-of-purchase displays, radio airplay, and live gig sales. In fact, many other uses for CDs will crop up after you start putting your promotional and sales machine to work.

Hard product is essential, even if you are only selling over the Internet. Many people do not have adequate digital players such as portable MP3 players or other digital "Walkman"-style players to play your music. Such people want to have a CD to play on a CD player, or even a cassette for the car cassette player.

That's why I feel it's important to cover the basics of manufacturing. Manufacturing is the process of taking your mixed recordings, and having them mastered into a form where they will be made into compact disks, cassettes, and/or vinyl (pressed records).

If you record dance music destined to be played in clubs, vinyl is still the best method for distributing copies to DJs for club play. If you are a trance, rave, disco, or techno artist, make sure you get at least 200 vinyl pressings of various mixes for the dance club market.

For the other forms of music, your main focus will be on having the majority of your music pressed to CDs. You'll need a small number of cassettes, if possible.

You'd be surprised at number of people who still buy cassettes. While cassette buyers do not make up a huge percentage of the music buying public, you should consider the cassette market if you can afford the additional costs necessary to have the artwork and printing done for cassettes.

The Cassette is still a popular format

There are a number of clever ways to save money on printing for your CDs and cassettes. Start with careful design, then use the services of a graphics artist or even a manufacturer offering graphic design and printing. You can accomplish a great look for less money than you would think, but high quality at a low price does take strategic planning to make it work.

Use designs that will double for posters. Create cassette inserts that can be used as mailers or lobby cards. Use everything you have at your fingertips to use "all the parts of the pig" without waste.

We won't get into extensive graphic design here. But it is important to mention that your package needs to look every bit as good as product being put out by the majors if you expect to be taken seriously.

The buying public is more sophisticated than you might think. When considering buying something from an unknown entity, the buyer is attracted by good design. Eye-catching clever design can go a long way toward making more sales.

Depending on your overall goals as a musician and recording artist, there are additional benefits arising from good packaging. Are you planning on going from an independent artist releasing product on your own label and selling direct, to actually signing a record deal? If so, then the impression you make on people in the record industry will count a great deal.

While designing the package, keep everyone in mind. Consider the clerks in the retail store taking your product on consignment. Consider everyone from those clerks up to big players in the industry who might be persuaded to sign you to a major contract. Your package must shine and stand out above the rest if you want everyone to give your package serious consideration as a contender.

You must remember that there are hundreds of thousands of artists out there. All of them are pitching product to any possible outlet, trying to get a deal and sell more product. Too many artists seem to cut corners in their packaging.

A word to the wise:

Do not skimp on your packaging. When you consider packaging, remember that packaging includes the manufacturing of your music.

You've come a long way and you've spent a lot of time and money to get your music to this point. Don't blow it by putting your valuable music in a shoddy, low fidelity vehicle.

Make no mistake about it. This is a business, and that business is about selling product, plain and simple. Nothing will mark you as an amateur more quickly than a product that does not look and sound as authentic as your competitor's product.

If you get nothing else from this section on manufacturing, or even this whole book, please take heed to the next paragraph.

> Your product must be competitively packaged and priced. It must be presented in the marketplace as equal to, if not better than, the product being released by the majors. With outstanding packaging, you can compete with the multinational corporation.

Packaging and the Internet

Now, you may be asking, what does packaging have to do with marketing direct on the Internet?

Everything, and here's why. Your product will be represented on the Internet not only as sound files, but also as graphics. Graphics include your album covers, CD art, promotional materials, everything you have from your band or artist, from photos down to the design of your lyric sheets. Make sure that all of these graphics bear the unmistakable imprint of a true professional.

In your online presentation, you do not have the advantage of to the person browsing in a retail store who may be able to physically examine your product by turning it in their hands. In your online presentation you must rely on showing your product in the most appealing and eye-catching way possible. You must appeal through your packaging, in particular, the elements of your packaging that are the graphics.

Of course, other elements are important too, including your Web site design, navigation, and promotional copy. But the main selling point, apart from the sound of your music, is your graphics package. Packaging, as they say, is everything.

We will first focus on the essential elements of your graphics, then address the manufacturing process.

Graphics

Graphics for your CD or cassette will generally consist of your cover and back cover art, your inserts, including lyric sheet, and whatever else you may decide to include. These extras might consist of a business reply card for your mailing list, a small catalog of your other records, or a merchandise catalog of other imprintables with your name, photo or logo on them. Some artists like to include a promotional poster, or incorporate this into a design that can also double as the cover.

Your first decision will be to decide the number of colors you want to use. If you decide to go with black and white, you will save money, but if you do this, make sure you get a graphic designer who really knows how to make black and white stand out.

If you prefer to go with color, keep in mind that the more colors you use, the more expensive the print job. There are innovative ways to use two color designs, but it may become necessary to go with four colors if your design requires it.

Four color printing can be expensive, because you are using a printing process that requires separate plates for each color. Although color separations can be done more cheaply with the advent of less expensive equipment, a really sharp four color separation and printing can also bring a higher price tag.

You should plan to press more CDs after you have sold out your first batch. Consider that plan when you order the print runs for your printed materials. You will save on printing if you print in one batch enough to use for your first and second pressings.

You'll be taking advantage of the fact that printing press setup is a large percentage of the cost of printing. Printing the covers for your first and second pressings in one print run requires only one printing press setup. So one run is much cheaper than printing the covers for the first and second pressings in two separate print runs.

Even if you are not sure if you will be able to sell your first batch of product, it's still better to get the extras printed. Printing extras will be inexpensive insurance. These printed materials can also serve well for promotional mailings, concert promotions, and other useful purposes beyond their primary uses as inserts. For an excellent source of additional uses for printed materials, refer to the index of books in the back of this book, or my Web site. You'll find more extensive information on the printing and packaging of your CDs.

The printed materials don't take much storage space. You can store the printed materials flat and they require no jewel cases until you are ready for your second batch of CDs. It would be a good idea to have them packed and sealed and away from moisture and heat until you need them.

Bar Coding

Since you will be placing your product with online retailers that require coding, you can see that bar coding is essential. To apply for a bar code, contact the Uniform Code Council. The cost is $300 to become a member, and this is a one-time fee.

You can reach them online at:

http://www.uc-council.org/

Bar codes help online retailers track inventory and payment data. Online partners such as Barnes and Noble, Amazon, and Borders all require bar coding on all products they carry. Finally, a bar code signifies you are not an amateur.

Brick and mortar record stores also require bar codes to monitor sales for chart action. One such monitoring program used by many retailers is Soundscan.

> **Brick and Mortar Stores**
> Physical stores in the real world

SoundScan is a firm that tracks music retail sales. If your product is sold in record stores and through distributors, with a proper bar code, chances are that SoundScan will be able to track it your sales.

Some record packaging companies, such as Diskmakers, offer free bar coding as a part of their package.

Pressing

The pressing or manufacturing plant you use is every bit as important as the recording studio you used to record your music. There are many pressing plants offering a variety of prices and services. It is up to you to find a manufacturer ready to do a quality job for you, at a sensible price.

I have used Diskmakers for years. They not only have reasonable prices for the quality they offer, they also have a complete packaging facility that can help you with your graphics as well as your mastering and pressing.

The people at Diskmakers are very friendly. They offer indie musicians a number of resources to help in getting the best quality master possible. They even help to market your music after it has been pressed.

Imprinted CDs are an option at Diskmakers

I recommend Diskmakers as a viable choice when doing your research on packaging, but do get information on other packagers, so that you can compare their pricing and services. See the discussion on Oasis later in this book for more packaging ideas.

Mastering

The first step in the process of preparing a CD is the mastering. When mastering you submit your final mixdown tape for preparation to be made into a final "master." The master will then be duplicated into the format you have chosen.

Mastering is often misunderstood, and its importance is almost always underestimated by the uninitiated. Preparing your final mix for mastering can make the difference between a great-sounding record and a mediocre one. At its best, a great master can transform your music into a sum greater than its parts; at its worst, a bad master can turn your beautifully mixed tracks into a muffled mess.

Mastering involves getting the final equalization perfect for reproduction. Sometimes this involves re-arranging the order of the songs for the perfect sequence, tweaking the compression, and likely a bit of magic that only the best mastering engineers secretly covet.

Don't be under the mistaken impression that because you recorded these songs yourself, you are safe, that your product needs no mastering. Often you must separate yourself from your baby, especially during this critical time. By using the services of a reputable mastering engineer, you will be giving your songs the best possible start in life.

Your manufacturer can often provide you with mastering services, if you ask for them. There is an extra charge for this service, but it is well worth it, if you do not know any good mastering engineers, or there are no mastering engineers readily available.

One question that arises is, how many CDs should you have pressed on your initial run? That is a difficult question, but the minimum is usually 1000. Your cost per unit goes down the more you get pressed. Conversely, if your number drops below 1000, your cost per unit rises. Since a profitable retail price depends on the cost of production, when you pay more per unit for pressing, you must charge more per unit. If you pressed fewer than 1,000, you would have to sell your product for a higher price than is competitive in order to make a profit.

Depending on your anticipated demand, you might well consider getting 1000-2000 more copies than expected.

If you are also selling your product from the stage during and after live performances, it is a good idea to have as many copies pressed as you can afford, without breaking the bank.

One low lost alternative to pressing large quantities of product is to purchase a CD burner and make limited quantities of your CDs yourself. Many of the CD-RW units are coming down in price, and include software that allow you to make your own covers and graphics.

Financing Your Pressing

There are many ways to raise or borrow money for your project. One relatively simple option is to set up a financing plan with your local bank or with your manufacturing facility.

Diskmakers offers a financing plan that allows you to pay for your manufacturing costs in installments. This is a great option if funds are tight, but you are serious about selling your CDs and you are willing to work hard.

By using such a plan, you can use the proceeds from selling your CDs to pay off your packaging costs. After you've paid your costs, the rest is profit.

But keep in mind you will be signing a legal document that holds you responsible for the repayment of the loan. This can create stress or even financial calamity if you don't sell enough to pay off your loan installments. For some, there is just no other way.

You may also be able to raise money among friends and family. Jana Stanfield suggests some really creative ways to approach such fundraising in her book *The Musician's Guide to Making & Selling Your Own CDs & Cassettes*.

Another way to raise money might be to locate investors online. This approach can take time, and requires a great deal of diligence and patience, but it can be done.

What you will be looking for is an "angel," or a silent investor who is willing to put up money and roll the dice on your group, or on your solo career.

Angels are not easy to find, and locating one who is in the music business and looking for a group to fund can be an arduous task. Proceed with caution when dealing with investors, and always hire the services of a good entertainment attorney before signing any agreements.

It is advisable, no matter which way you go, to have a business plan. A professionally written business plan shows investors that you are serious about your business. The business plan is also one more step toward a professional presentation.

Finding Money Online

There are a number of online listing services that help to match investors with projects. Here are three:

Capital Connection
http://capital-connection.com/entrepapponline.html

VentureSeek
http://www.ventureseek.com

The Investor's Network
http://www.investorsnet.com/

Low Cost Alternatives to Recording And Pressing

When you are first getting started, money can be the most difficult hurdle of all. Recording and pressing your product cost money. Yet, you need product in order to make money.

A low cost way to record your product is to purchase a used portable 4 track cassette recorder. I have had amazingly good results in my experiments with these units, and you can locate a used 4 track for as low as $100. When buying one of these units used, make sure it includes some type of noise reduction, equalization for each channel, and has limited head wear.

You can find higher-end digital recording units inexpensively online such as at recycler.com, or refurbished units from your local electronics dealer.

Using a 4 track can be a real challenge. Yet for a singer-songwriter or a band recording "live" in the studio, excellent results can be obtained with careful planning and submixing.

I highly recommend a high quality microphone. If you cannot afford the best, you can get acceptable results from the Radio Shack Pro-Unidirectional "High-Ball" microphone, catalog number 33-984, for $59.95.

With a little ingenuity, you can accomplish a great deal without spending huge amounts of money, and you can still get great results. But eventually, you must move up to the next level and do it at the highest quality you can afford.

3
Choosing Your Marketing Plan

Any online marketing plan should be backed up with an offline sales strategy. Your efforts will yield greater results when using online and offline methods together. Offline marketing is a book in itself, and beyond the scope of our discussion here, but I will mention several offline areas where you can focus your efforts to maximize your online plan.

First and foremost, your live appearances are extremely important in terms of boosting online sales. Many artists feel that they can sell their music exclusively online, and many do. However, the majority of successful independent artists do live gigs to sell their records, in addition to maintaining a strong Web presence.

I'm not saying you can't sell records without playing live, you just won't sell as many.

Secondly, when you are not playing live, you should advertise your online site in every way you can. Use bumper stickers, license plate holders, T-shirts, giveaways. Even a magnetic sign on a car door can work wonders.

One method I find very effective is one of those programmable signs that scroll red letters across a diode screen. These can be hooked up to the back window of your car, and wired into the auto power. The sign gets attention and can be easily read during the day, but it really attracts the eye at night. You can program the sign with your sales message and URL. These signs can be picked up used for under $100.

A Word about Web Technology

This book assumes you have mastered the basics of getting onto the Internet and using a browser. You should have at least a rudimentary knowledge of how Web pages and files work.

It also assumes you know the Internet basics, what a search engine does, and the elementary principles of communicating on the Web, such as e-mail.

If you do not have these basics, I would recommend the excellent book, *Internet For Dummies* by John R. Levine, Margaret Levine Young, and Carol Baroudi. (available in online bookstores and through my Web site.)

Methods of Marketing Online

Once you've completed your CD, and your artwork is done, it's time to get the word out.

Step #1 Get Your Own Domain Name and Web site

The first and most important tool in your arsenal is your own Web site, with its own unique URL or address. I'm not talking about a home page that you might get free through AOL, Mindspring, or one of those cheap hosts that load you on their server with ten thousand other people.

I'm talking about registering your own unique domain name, like elvis.com. Then your URL will be http://www.elvis.com. You want a domain name with your name, your company, or your group name in the title.

This will be your own Web address. After you register the domain name, it's yours to keep as long as you keep your name registration current.

It costs very little to register your own domain name for a year through one of the various name registries. My company, New Media Digital, will register the domain name free for clients who sign up with our hosting company. Which brings us to the topic of Web hosting services.

Step #2 Find A Good Web Host

A hosting company provides you with a space on their server, and that space will be where your domain, or Web site, resides. There are local hosts, national hosts, even hosts in other countries where you can have your site hosted.

But you only need one Web host. After you find a good Web host and they install your site on their server, your site will be accessible from every online computer in the world. People will access your site simply by typing in the URL the domain name you have registered.

There are many Web hosts, but not all are reliable. It is important that you find a good reliable Web hosting company, a company ready to give you personalized service.

Some of the larger Web hosts treat you as just one of the many bees in the hive. They leave you feeling faceless and left on permanent hold when you need help. This is not good if your site is down, or your e-mail is not working, or you have one of several problems that can arise.

I've been in the hosting service business for six years now, and I've heard all the horror stories. People tell me about getting with hosts whose servers are always breaking down, slow, or just unreachable much of the time.

Yes, it's true that a top notch host may cost an extra $25 a month in hosting fees, but isn't that worth the peace of mind and the extra sales you'll make because people can reach your site immediately?

There are places to be thrifty, but your hosting is not one of them. In this digital age, surfers don't wait around for pages to load. As soon as a surfer types in your URL or clicks your link, your pages must come up. Fast. Anything less is unacceptable, because you will lose customers and money if you do not use a reliable host.

Generally, a small business Web site that can handle all of your needs for selling your album, including e-commerce (taking credit cards), playing audio and video clips, and providing space for photos and text and multiple pages, can be had for about $50 per month.

Step #3 Set Up E-Commerce

In order to sell your CD online, you'll need some way to take the orders and collect the money. Accepting credit cards is the best way to take orders over the net, and the most popular.

Online shopping using credit cards has gained worldwide acceptance. Secure transactions are now considered the norm, and the fear of doing business online with a credit card has virtually disappeared.

E-commerce solutions come in many varieties. You can choose among the various possibilities:

1. Use a secure interactive online order form and accept credit cards using your own credit card merchant account. Apply for a merchant account and get special software to process the transactions yourself, either automatically or manually.

2. Use a secure interactive online order form and accept credit cards using someone else's credit card merchant account. Get a third party processor to handle the sale for a small percentage of the sale.

3. Use a secure interactive online order form and accept online checks. Use online check processing software.

4. Use a printable online order form. Have the buyer print out the order form, fill out the form, and send you a check through the mail with the printed order form.

Some vendors prefer to have a special merchant account set up with software that will process a customer's card right from the Web site, so they do not have to pay a third party billing service.

But keep in mind that the set up fees and software, coupled with "chargeback" and processing fees, can eat up what small profit margin you have.

At this writing, Internet merchants are not protected from chargebacks. This means that if you sell a customer a product online and use their credit card number to process the sale, the person can later come back and claim they never received the merchandise.

If you have not taken a "hard swipe" of the card, then you would have to refund the money. This is true even if you had a receipt that the buyer paid. You would also have to pay a bank chargeback fee, usually $10-$20 per transaction, in addition to the refund. This means that if you sold a CD for $15, and the buyer refuted the credit card charge, you would lose the $15. You would also lose the shipping, and you would pay the bank fee, so you would go in the hole on the sale.

There is another disadvantage to using your own merchant account. If your chargebacks reach over 1%, your merchant bank could pull your account without warning, leaving you suddenly without any way to process orders.

The reasons for this policy by Visa and Mastercard are many, but there's no doubt about the fact that it's unfair to online merchants. There are currently lobbies in Washington trying to come up with a system that will protect the merchant, but there has been nothing resolved.

You might consider using a third-party billing service to set up a special sales shopping cart system for you, in exchange for 15% of the sale. You may find a service worthwhile when you consider all that they offer.

Why? Because dealing with online credit cards can become a chore.

Third-party billing services can often protect you from chargebacks, and in some cases will not charge you a bank fee if a chargeback is made.

Another great advantage to third party billing is that some of the better ones use sophisticated "scrub" systems that can run a potential customer's credit card through a database to see if there is any chargeback or fraud activity on their card. (For a list of third party billing companies, please see Appendix 1 in the back of this book.)

Step #4 Design your Site for Marketing

Setting up e-commerce is not enough. Your Web site must be truly geared to marketing, making it easy for the visitor to understand your offer and order your music.

Your Web Site Design

A great deal can be written about the design of your Web site. You can hire a professional Web design firm to create one for you, or you can build one yourself.

Your Web site is your presentation to the world. Don't skimp on it, it is a vitally important step in the marketing and sales process. Your Web site must be fast loading, clean, easy to navigate, and professional.

There are a lot of programs out there that make it pretty simple to build your own pages. The simpler ones use a method called 'WYSIWYG,' which stands for What You See is What You Get.' These programs work on principles similar to a word processor, but with advanced graphics functions.

After selecting a color for the background of your Web page, you simply type your text. As you type, whatever appears on the screen is actually written in HTML code, or Web language, behind what you are typing.

There are also Web design programs and places online that can help you build your Web site using templates and drag-and-drop interfaces that will allow you to place graphics and other elements right into your pages.

It is very important to make a good first impression on your customer. That's why we recommend you spend the extra money and have a professional Web design firm create your Web site for you. Preferably, find one that is familiar with music retailing on the net, or you may find yourself paying for a Web site that does not do an effective selling job.

Your Web site should be fun and informative, with plenty of navigation buttons and a clean, easy to load, easy to read interface.

Some of the music portals offer you a Web page, but it is important to also have your own, because you want to be able to sell your music directly from your own Web site. Your own Web site casts a more professional impression on your clients than a simple sub-page on a music portal.

Your Web site should be designed to maximize the likelihood of people being able to find you on all the major search engines.

A professional Web design firm will be able to maximize your pages for these engines by the strategic placement of "meta tags." Meta tags are special codes in the Web pages containing keywords and page descriptions. The meta tags help to inform the search engines on the topics covered by your pages and thus, where your pages should be listed, and their relevance to a given search.

Building Web pages and maximizing them for your marketing efforts can be a daunting, complicated process. By paying a professional design firm, you free up your time for the actual marketing. But if money is extremely tight, you might do well to learn everything you can about the building of Web pages and how to place meta tags on the pages. By doing it yourself, you not only save money, but you learn a vital skill applicable to your future marketing efforts.

The science of search engines is a constantly evolving one, but we will cover how they work and their functions on our section of search engines.

Your Web site should impress upon your prospective customer that you are a person who cares about your business. The Web site should cast the impression that you are on top of your game, and should also encourage the visitor to play your music. This will, in turn, entice him to buy.

Beware the Hard Sell

Always ask for the sale, but be careful of the hard sell. Too much push will send your customer fleeing. Getting sales is a bit like fishing. Use good bait. Have patience. And when the fish bites, don't move too fast to reel him in, but give him leeway.

If he wants to leave without buying, that's cool. It's going to happen much of the time. But if every surfer leaves without buying, you may need to tweak your pages a bit. If tweaking doesn't help, seek the advice of a Web marketing consultant to make sure your pages are the best they can be.

Mainly, let the customer make the value judgment to buy or not. If you have done your job, you will have made a stellar presentation, and given him plenty of information on which to base his decision.

If nothing else, you have let him know you are there, and that presence can be worth a great deal. Your presence leads to what marketing experts call "product awareness."

Capturing the E-Mail Address

A vital part of your Web site design is to include a way for your prospects to contact you for more information. One excellent way to do this is to create an "opt-in" newsletter, to keep the fans up to date on your latest activities. By opt-in, we mean that people choose to be on your newsletter e-mailing list.

You can include info about your live appearances, new song creation, recording activities, your new CDs, even personal info about what's going on in your life. (Be careful about discussing your life, and make sure you keep the tone upbeat.)

Once you capture an e-mail address, you have a direct pipeline to your fan base. This is your bread and butter! Don't abuse it with daily mailings. Rather, send a monthly or bi-weekly bulletin on your activities.

One important consideration, however, is the climate of a thing called "spam." Many Internet users are tired of being inundated with unsolicited e-mail, and will complain to their system administrators if they receive e-mail they have not requested.

> **Spam**
> Unsolicited commercial e-mail sent to a large number of recipients

Sending unsolicited "bulk" e-mail is an activity that can turn your prospective fans into enemies and get your site shut down permanently. Despite what you may read about the effectiveness of this form of marketing, don't believe it. "Spam" is bad news, and you must always avoid spamming.

So how do you capture e-mail addresses? By placing a simple box or announcement on your front page, with a little sign up box, that reads something like: "Sign up for my monthly newsletter and keep up on what I'm doing!"

This is where people sign on to join the opt-in list. When a fan signs up for your newsletter, an opt-in program will send an e-mail to the fan asking them to confirm their subscription to your mailings.

This program also allows them to "opt-out" whenever they wish, so that if the mailings become bothersome, or they just don't wish to receive them anymore, a simple *Remove* or *Unsubscribe* request sent through e-mail will trigger the program to automatically remove their e-mail address from the database.

The beauty of this technique is that you know that every person on your mailing list has requested your mailings and confirmed his request. The people on your list want to hear from you, so they are 100% qualified to hear your sales message.

In the marketing world, such a list is worth its weight in gold. The great value of an opt-in e-mail list is the reason why portal sites that gather e-mail info and subsequent demographic data can sell their sites for millions of dollars.

There are many different mailing list programs you can use, and some of the programs are free. I like using a program called Listbot, which is an online mailing list subscriber management tool. Listbot allows you to manage your lists efficiently, using all kinds of great features. The program is also free, so the price is right.

You can access their site and check out the program at: http://www.listbot.com

Addresses For Success

The many MP3-type portal sites some of the most important places to get your site listed. These portal sites attract large numbers of fans looking for free music downloads.

Some of these sites offer you your own home page, where fans can go and check out what you have to offer. Most of the portal sites that do not charge for this service will want a piece of your sales action.

Over the course of time as you become more popular, you may want to become more selective regarding your partner sites. For now, you will want to list with as many portals as possible.

There are also premium portal sites that attract large numbers of fans. These premium sites will charge you a rental fee per month, and they will help market your site and music to a large number of users.

For instance, the portal Free Music-Planet.com places a select number of musicians on this site. The site charges a small monthly fee for the rental space ($50), but does not take any percentage of sales.

Says site administrator Brian Davis, "I feel the musician should reap the rewards for their music, especially when they are willing to invest a small amount of rental income to their Web space. We like to think of it as renting retail space in a mall. The mall brings in the crowds, and the retailer gets to keep all the profits."

In addition to a home page and free advertising on the site, Free-Music Planet also offers an additional free listing in their online MP3 search engine. They offer deep discounts on advertising, free consultations, and marketing tools to help maximize sales and reaching larger audiences. Examples of such tools include the ability to do live Web broadcasts or participate in exclusive portal radio stations.

Many music portal sites even offer a way to network with other musicians who are marketing their music direct to the consumer. Networking musicians can share tips and tricks while offering encouragement and support. Such networking is done through bulletin boards, chat rooms, and newsletters.

"Not all portal sites are created equal," says Sherry Rockets, of the pop-rock group Jiffy-Pop. "We've had trouble with payouts from one of the largest portals out there, and there is virtually no customer service."

"That is why we choose to not work with sites that burn CDs for us for a percentage of the profits. We simply direct them from our free downloads to our own Web site, and make the sale from there."

The growing pains which accompany new businesses, particularly in a new industry, are not lost in the online portal world. This is why it is important to have your own Web site, in addition to listing with the portal sites. The exposure these portal sites can bring is vital, especially to a new artist. But you shouldn't rely on portal sites exclusively to sell your product.

Step #5 Four Prongs to Music Marketing Success

Your effective marketing plan for music involves a four-prong process:

1. Online Live

2. Online Media

3. Offline Live

4. Offline Media

By approaching your marketing on multiple fronts, each front will support the others and add momentum to your sales.

Remember that the idea behind any marketing is to create product awareness by getting information in front of as many people as possible. This must be done on all four fronts to make it kick ass.

I will cover each of the four prongs in the next four chapters.

4
Prong 1:
Online Live Marketing

Here we begin our chapters on the Four Prongs To Music Marketing Success.

Online "live" has a double meaning. Online live first means making live appearances online, performing, going to bulletin boards and chat rooms, and doing live Web-radio interviews. Online live also involves posting information about your site to other sites.

Here are some of the methods to use in Prong 1.

Posting to Bulletin Boards

The Web offers thousands of bulletin boards aimed at fans of new music. The boards are usually organized under a specific music type, like trance, rave, country, metal, goth, and so on. These bulletin boards are frequented by people who love a specific kind of music. These people form a niche market of targeted prospective buyers.

Music bulletin board interface

The idea is to go into these bulletin board areas and post a message like:

"If anyone here is looking for new free music, we want to tell you about us, the screaming slingblades. We are a hot new metal group giving away free downloads of our latest releases, Metallica-driven originals to die for!

http://www.yourdomain.com"

Now you don't have to use that specific post, but you get the idea. It's conversational in tone, but it gets the message across.

Now some bulletin boards, as well as chat rooms (the distinction is that chat rooms are live) are moderated. Moderated boards and rooms forbid any kind of commercial advertising. Usenet Newsgroups also forbid advertising.

In a situation like this, you must be more subtle in your approach. You might try something like:

"Hi I am a heavy metal guitarist looking to get some feedback from fellow guitarists and fans about my music. I invite you to visit my site and listen to my music, I'd love to hear your ideas and opinions."

Then you can either list your URL, or you can put it in your signature file.

For those of you who are not familiar with the signature file, or "sig file," it is a four line tag you place at the bottom of every e-mail you send. The sig file contains information that identifies you, and it usually includes your name, URL, e-mail address, and sometimes the name of your group or business.

The sig file is universally accepted Web-wide as a non-intrusive way to get the word out without being too blatant. The sig file can be set up to appear automatically at the bottom of your text when you send or answer e-mail, and sometimes when you post to bulletin boards.

Some bulletin boards require that you sign up with them to obtain a unique user name and password. This cuts down on wandering spammers who just want to crash the bulletin board with unwanted advertisements.

Another great advantage to secure bulletin boards is that some offer some nice bells and whistles. The Home Recording bulletin board is one such example. You can elect to have an e-mail automatically sent to you to inform you as soon as someone answers your post. This notification tells you that someone has responded so that you can log on and read the response. This service is enormously helpful for many applications.

The Home Recording Web site is also a tremendous resource. You can check them out at:

http://www.homerecording.com/

One very good source for music bulletin boards, broken down into style, is:

http://www.imusic.com/bbs/

Participating in Chat Rooms

One of the most popular pastimes online is chat. It is one of the reasons why chat is one of the most requested keywords online (below MP3). Use chat rooms in a variety of places to engage users in conversations about your music. If you approach it in a sincere way, you'll find people will quite often support your efforts.

One guerrilla tactic is called the "drive-by spamming." This is where you place a message in your clipboard, essentially an ad, and go to a large chat area ·such as Yahoo Chat! The drive-by involves switching rooms as quickly as possible and dropping your message into as many conversations as possible.

This works to some extent, but I would stay away from it. First of all, it's bad netiquette. You are trying to build a long term audience and a dedicated fan base, not tick people off. If you try the approach of sincerity, you will have a more loyal following that will pay large dividends in the long run.

Secondly, the drive by can get you banned from certain chat areas, and while it's easy enough to change your login name, it is tough to disguise yourself when you drop your message "bomb" proclaiming to everyone you are, in fact, the same spammer under a different guise.

The most effective approach to chat room marketing is: be honest and be interested in what others have to say. You should frequent chat rooms populated by people in your demographic and music style.

Yes, it takes time. But it all takes time. Remember, you are building your fan base, one customer at a time. One customer could be a customer for life.

There are lots of chat rooms dedicated to specific interests, and that is where your niche market waits. Some very good chat areas to try are:

http://chat.yahoo.com/

http://www.chatplanet.com/

http://www.worldvillage.com/wv/chat/html/chat.htm

http://www.chat-rooms.com/

Yahoo's Music Chatrooms draw big audiences

You may also want to consider getting an account with AOL. America Online has the largest installed base of Internet users in the world. They have an extensive selection of chat rooms, and if you frequent them on evenings and weekends, you can reach thousands of people, and send hundreds of visitors to your Web site. More visitors means more sales!

Using Usenet Newsgroups

If you've never been to Usenet, go now. It is the largest collection of special interest discussion groups in the world. Unlike a chat room, Usenet works more like a bulletin board, where users all over the world can go to a special topic group and post relevant discussion threads.

> **To Go to Usenet**
> http://groups.google.com

The subjects are as far-reaching and diverse as the stars in the sky. You are looking for the special interest groups pertaining to your particular style of music. You may also want to consider starting a newsgroup of your own.

For a thorough look at what Usenet is (and isn't) I am reprinting (with his permission of course) an article by Chip Salzenberg. You can read the full article in Appendix 3.

One of the biggest problems with Usenet as a marketing vehicle is that although the rules state it is not to be used for commercial purposes, many people spam the groups, creating a tremendous strain on the system. Users wishing to pursue topics of interest must often wade through hundreds of spam messages for pornographic sites, get rich quick schemes, and other such items. It makes Usenet a difficult place to get your message heard.

One way to approach this challenge would be to start your own moderated newsgroup, or to post only to newsgroups which have a moderator. These moderators act as "watchdogs," making sure that inappropriate posts never get posted. The downside, of course, is that you are limited to using your sig file as the only means of promotion, because more blatant ads will cause you to be removed.

However, Usenet remains one of the most effective free methods of reaching a worldwide targeted audience. The sheer volume of people who access Usenet as a special interest vehicle makes it an ideal place to spread the word about your music.

You can participate in the discussion threads in targeted market groups. By participating, you inform those who love your type of music that an exciting new group or artist is just appearing on the horizon. These targeted readers will be delighted to hear that free music is only a click away.

In this regard, approach Usenet with the same concern for netiquette as you would bulletin boards and chat rooms.

Usenet Tips and Tricks

When marketing on Usenet, you can try different formats. One format is the *press release*, where you are simply making an announcement about your band or music in press release format:

FOR IMMEDIATE USENET RELEASE

Mark W. Curran, the folk-rock troubadour, has just released his new CD on New Media Digital Records. The CD contains 12 original songs, and are available for free download and review at his site at http://www.markcurran.com

"I am very happy about the release of my latest songs," Curran announced at a recent Los Angeles press conference.

For more information about the CD, please contact the artist at:

http://www.markcurran.com

"30"

Although the press release is a form of advertising, it is acceptable for many Usenet groups. Try using that format, and check the newsgroups through different dial-up connections to make sure that the post has propagated.

Headlines and ID Tags

Your post will initially be seen only as an ID tag and a headline. This will be your only chance to grab the viewer's attention and get him to click on your post to read it. Use it well.

The ID line is for a return e-mail address.

The ID Line and headline look something like this:

your-e-mail@musicman.com NEW CD JUST RELEASED!

I personally do not like to place my own e-mail address in the ID tag. The reason for this is I don't want spammers using my e-mail address to send me junk mail. If you post a lot to Usenet, and you use your own e-mail address, you will eventually be flooded with unwanted mail. I also feel using an e-mail address is a waste of valuable space, when it could be used to further your goal of arousing the viewer's curiosity.

One of the most powerful words in marketing is the word FREE. You can use it in your ID line as well as your headline:

freemusic@fm.comFREE Gothic-Rock Downloads NOW

If you come up with an appealing headline like the above, you can write it in the form of a press release, or you can make it conversational in tone. One trick is to write it as a reply to a previous thread:

Mookie,

Regarding your post, I found one such group that does gothic-metal in much the same vein as Ozzie Osborne. They are called the Bloody Switchblades and I got their free download at: http://www.bloodyswitchblades.com.

see ya

Trump

If you really want to get clever, you can keep your eye out for posts or threads from people who are actually looking for the type of music you offer, and then reply to it using your promo info in a conversational reply.

Another trick is to use one ID to post a question, and then post a reply using a different alias. This might look something like this:

Post Question:

Where can I find Ozzie type gothic free?

- Rigormortis@rg.com

Reply to thread:

I found Ozzie gothic for FREE!

You can find it at http://www.bloodyswitchblades.com. This is a great site for this kind of goth.

- Joanne Pierce

In other words, you have started a thread, or subject, under one alias and then answered your own post with a different alias.

To track the results of any given post, you can set up *doorway pages* with counters on them, and key each post to a different doorway page. By checking your page hit counters daily, you can track which ads or posts pull the best.

Like any form of marketing, working Usenet involves a great deal of patience and diligence. Utilizing this marketing method for only one hour, three days per week, you can achieve excellent results.

For more tips and tricks on using Usenet as a marketing tool, go to:

http://www.1stpositions.com/guerilla/newsgrou.html

One word of caution: spamming Usenet, or breaking the rules of netiquette by posting inappropriate messages containing blatant sales and advertising pitches can not only get you banned from that newsgroup, but can also result in your losing your Internet connection.

ISP's frown on spam, no matter what flavor it is, and they have an especially low tolerance for Usenet spam. When complaints happen, they happen in volume, resulting in a tirade of angry *flamers* sending mail bombs, complaints, and other such hassles to not only you, but also to your system administrator.

In extreme cases, the flamers also send complaints to the uplink or backbone provider, the companies who supply the local ISP with his phone line leasing. When complaints start coming down the line from the top of the food chain, local ISPs have little choice other than to remove your from their system.

Stay within the rules, and you'll find Usenet a rewarding marketing method that should not be ignored. For a detailed discussion of marketing through newsgroups, read Mark Joyner's article in Appendix 4.

Link Exchanges

One of the more established methods of getting traffic to your site is the link exchange. The idea here is to find sites that are similar to your own, and request to list their site on yours, and you will do the same for them.

For instance, if you have a folk group, go to other folk group sites and request a link exchange. Find out if the site accepts a plain text link, and/or a banner link. If they accept banners, you can send them your banner and they will put it up in their links area, and you will do the same for them.

By establishing a special page for links, and setting up a link to it from your home page is good business, and also gives your visitors a chance to go to other sites that are similar to yours.

It is good business to exchange links, and keeps the synergy going while not wasting traffic that might otherwise go elsewhere.

It also brings fresh new qualified traffic to your own site, which results in sales.

The more sites you can exchange links with, the better and wider your exposure. But it is always a good idea to check the sites you are exchanging links with, to make sure your reciprocal link stays up.

You may find some sites may remove your link if you are not sending much return traffic. If this occurs, simply remove this person's link from your links area.

You might also want to trade links with resource sites put up by other indie artists. This works best if you put up a resource page of your own. A resource page is a list of links indie artists may find helpful in promoting their music.

Search Engines

One of the most misunderstood areas of online marketing is the search engine area. For our marketing efforts, we need to be concerned with the top ten majors, which are currently:

Yahoo	Open Directory Project
LookSmart	Excite
AltaVista	MSN Search
Lycos	Google
Webcrawler	AllTheWeb

One unfortunate trend we have seen in recent months is the move of some of the major search engines toward charging money to consider your site for inclusion in their indexes.

Yahoo began this trend, charging a whopping $200 to merely consider a site for inclusion in their commercial categories.

If your site is selling anything, it's considered commercial. And Yahoo will not even guarantee a listing! In fact, they will keep your $200 even if they don't list you. In our opinion, this is highway robbery.

Ever quick to make even larger profits than they are already making off their advertisers, other major search engines have begun to follow Yahoo's lead, offering a "Business Class", or "Express Submit" listing service.

How many search engines will adopt this practice, and how many will drop it due to public outcry, remains to be seen. As of this writing, Yahoo is the only search engine that requires payment to consider listing your site.

Alta Vista and Webcrawler offer a "Express Listing" service for $199, but still offer their standard submission option, suggesting it could take "weeks" to appear in their indexes.

There are a few ways around the Yahoo roadblock. I've heard some musicians submit their sites as personal Web sites. They start by offering nothing for sale, and wait till they get listed, then place their CDs up once they start getting traffic.

Unethical?

In my opinion, no more unethical than the practice of charging $199 for simply considering your site and not returning your money if they don't list you.

Another method I've heard used is that you can submit your commercial site for consideration to Yahoo, and if they pull a fast one on you and don't list you and try to keep your money, charge back the charge on your credit card statement.

I can't say I agree with either one of these practices, because two wrongs don't make a right, so you will have to use your own judgement on this. I cannot advise you in this area, but I will say that if you disagree with Yahoo's practice of charging money for merely looking at your site, write the Federal Trade Commission and start making some waves about it.

There are many categories to list your site under in Yahoo, and what constitutes "commercial" is a slippery slope that you may be able to skirt by submitting to the appropriate category.

I will explain how each of these search engines works, but first, an overview of the process. There are two basic types of search engines.

1. hand-indexed
2. spider-indexed

Some search engines are hand-indexed, meaning that when you submit your Web site to them for review, a human goes to your site. This human reviewer clicks on the links and rates the site for relevancy under the category you selected when you submitted the site.

Automated, or spider-based search engines send out a software robot that cruises through your Web pages. The robot rates your pages for keyword relevancy, adding up the number of repeated phrases, subjects, and similar links to arrive at a sophisticated deduction that will determine the ranking of your site in their database.

Each of the search engines have algorithms and criteria that are constantly changing. The search engines are trying to keep ahead of those who try to fool the engines into giving them a ranking higher than warranted by the content of their pages.

To keep up with the latest search engine technology, changes, methods, and updates, visit:

http://www.searchenginewatch.com/

Maximizing Your Pages for Search Engines

One of the most important marketing methods is to keyword maximize your pages so that the search engines can find you when people type in certain keywords. One optimization method uses meta tags. You should create meta tags within the context of your page, then place them within the HEAD tags on the page. Such meta tags can help increase your ranking considerably.

Learning to use meta tags and maximizing your pages to rank best in each search engine is a science in itself. It's a skill well worth learning if you are to increase your chances of survival and increase sales.

Because the search engine algorithms are always changing, you must continually devise new ways to rank higher on the engines. The only way to do this is to study the search engines, and to visit resource sites like Search Engine Watch to find out the latest on what works.

One trick is to research your competition. Go to a search engine and type in your most important keyword. This is the keyword you want people to search on to find your site in the search engine listings. From the search engine listings for that keyword, follow the link to each page appearing in the Top 20. Look at the page in the browser and use the View menu Source option to evaluate the meta tags. Analyze the aspects of these pages that resulted in their superior ranking. Then try to duplicate the methods the top sites have used. But don't copy any page. It is not a good idea to copy someone's code, because that is, in essence, stealing.

Another thing to remember is that the page you now see may not be the page that got the ranking in the first place. Savvy Webmasters who know the tricks or have stumbled onto them by accident will often get their ranking and switch out the page that got them there, so that nobody else can copy their method.

But not all the pages that have achieved their ranking have been switched. You can be sure that a good many of the pages you view in the top 20 of the major ten search engines are the actual pages that achieved the original ranking. Accordingly, you can study those pages for ideas.

Creating doorway pages is a good method for getting ranked on spider-based search engines. A doorway page is a page that contains a number of phrases and keywords that center around a targeted search term. For instance, if you want to rank high under the phrase "free heavy metal music," then you might use this phrase in a number of sentences, repeating the phrase throughout the page.

Beware, that if you overdo it, and don't achieve the proper balance for that particular engine, you could be penalized by that engine for violating the rules. The usual penalty is to be omitted from the search engine's listings completely.

It's a tricky balance, but you can achieve high rankings with diligent and persistent effort. I recommend making doorway pages each day, and submitting them to the different spider-based engines.

As for the hand-indexed engines, submission is tougher. With hand-indexed engines, you have to be continually creating new pages that have relevance to your keywords. A good way to do this is to write short articles of 300 words or less, and name the page to reflect the keywords you are trying to rank under. Every time you write a new article, target a different keyword or phrase, and then submit that page to the engines.

Also, make sure to list your site and songs on all the major music search engines. The majors are:

SongSpyder
http://www.songspyder.com/

Napster
http://www.napster.com/

Gnutella
http://gnutella.wego.com/

Lycos / FAST MP3 Search
http://mp3.lycos.com/

MP3.com
http://mp3.com/

MP3meta
http://www.mp3meta.com/
Search all the major MP3 search engines at once through this metasearch service from SavvySearch.

AudioGalaxy
http://www.audiogalaxy.com/

Arianna MP3
http://mp3.iol.it
Italian MP3 search engine.

Getsongs - MP3 Search Engines
http://altern.org/getsongs
Query multiple MP3 search engines from one place.

AudioPhilez
http://www.audiophilez.com
Displays technical info about each song listed in search results.

Manic Music
http://www.m-music.net
Lets you choose to search from many MP3 search engines, though only one at a time.

Dgolpe
http://www.dgolpe.com
Directory of downloads specializing in Latin and world music.

2Look4
http://www.2look4.com/

Oth.net
http://oth.net/

Audiofind
http://www.audiofind.com/

Eisbaer.org
http://www.eisbaer.org
Dutch-based MP3 search engine.

Soundcrawler
http://www.soundcrawler.com

MediaLeech search
http://medialeech.m4d.com/

Be sure to read Appendix 5 for Search Engine Placement Tips by search engine guru Danny Sullivan.

Online Promotions

Have you ever noticed how successful radio stations and retail stores are always attracting media attention and customers? They usually do it by the vehicle of promotions.

These are essentially giveaways designed to attract a crowd. Merchandisers and marketers alike know the most powerful word in the sales arsenal is the word FREE, and they use it for maximum power.

In much the same way as brick and mortar companies use promotions such as giveaways, so will you. One way to do this is to set up a free CD giveaway. Of course, your own CD will be the central giveaway, but since your own CD may not have the drawing power required, you need to set up some bait.

A bait CD might be for a popular group in your genre. For example, if you are a rock group, and your music is quite similar or would sell to the same fan base as Mettallica's, perhaps you would purchase 10 Metallica CDs.

Then you would contact a popular online radio station and offer to set up a free promotional concert, featuring your group, and offer to do free giveaways live on the air. The content of this show would be interviews, live performance, perhaps even a Web cam stream.

There's no end to the many ways you can use this basic premise as the anchor for your online promotions. You can set up e-mail or call-in contests to guess at rock trivia questions. You can use humor, perhaps tying into a recent scandal or media headline.

For instance, during the Clinton-Lewinsky scandal, our company contacted a popular online radio station and ran an online lie detector test with a Bill Clinton soundalike. In between, we ran live and recorded music programming for one of our clients. The result was quite effective and brought us decent sales.

Online radio stations love this kind of thing because it attracts attention, gives them free promotion, and also gives them free content. It can also be used with offline media, such as with local college radio stations.

Mailing Lists

The most important tool in the arsenal is your mailing list. Your objective is to start and build an opt-in e-mail subscriber list. I covered the basics of getting e-mail addresses from your home page, in my section "Capturing The E-Mail Address." Here I will delve into more methods to get them.

The mailing list goes hand in hand with your newsletter. By creating a monthly mailing on a given topic, you can, under the guise of information, send your promotions to everyone on your mailing list.

Capturing the e-mail address for your opt-in list, you send a monthly newsletter via e-mail. It doesn't have to be a literary masterpiece. In fact, the shorter and simpler the newsletter, the better.

Anyone who is in your target market is a potential opt-in subscriber, and as such, a buying customer in the making. The best ways to capture the e-mail address is from a form on your Web page, and a signup sheet at all of your promotions.

To get new addresses, your posts to Usenet will bring traffic to your site, where a percentage will sign up for your opt-in list. This also holds true for all the traffic you have directed from other sites, including the portal sites like MP3.com

Remember that the only real acceptable and usable mailing list is an opt-in list, whereby each subscriber has taken a two-step verification process to join your subscriber base. This means that buying e-mail addresses is out of the question. Such lists are not made up of opt-in subscribers. If someone is offering such a list, they are either scamming you or they are betraying the trust of the members of an existing subscriber list.

Subscribers on such a list would not be open to receiving unsolicited mail from you, even if they are your target group. Getting new e-mail addresses is done by the development of the next tool, the e-mail newsletter.

E-Mail Newsletters

An e-mail newsletter goes out each month to your subscriber base. You can start an e-mail newsletter on any topic of relevance to your target audience. The first and most common, is the newsletter that gives updates on what is happening with your group, your latest recordings, appearances, Web activity, and so on.

The second type is genre specific. For example, if you are a Heavy Metal group, you might consider putting out a newsletter of interest to Heavy Metal fans. This newsletter might cover the national scene, popular groups, the indie scene, or one particular group or artist.

The newsletter might even be targeted to a more specific sub-genre, like gothic or grunge, perhaps punk. The idea here is to target the newsletter to the type of audience your music targets. Then you can slip your promotional messages in between the latest news and gossip.

Here is a sample page from a newsletter:

Heavy Metal Monthly

The Barflys appeared at The Lowdown Club last week, and the SRO crowd went nuts during the band's sixty minute set.

The latest release from Grunge-O-Mat hits music stores on Friday, a company spokesman said today in a press conference held by Warner Brothers Records.

Are you looking for great Heavy Metal? Come to: http://www.yoursite.com

We've got free downloads and more free offers and giveaways. Find out how to win free tickets to our next show!

(More news and info here)

The newsletter should not run on for pages. It should be kept short and concise. One surefire method to get subscribers of your opt-in list to come to your Web site is by starting a hot story in the newsletter. Then place a "continued here" hyperlink to your Web site. The readers will then click on the link to read the rest of the story.

This trick will save you newsletter space, and it cuts down on clutter. This trick also gives you an opportunity to place your sales message on the page they see after clicking on the link.

Newsletter & Discussion Group Management Sites

Newsletters and discussion groups are often synonymous, but I call any mailing to a subscriber list a newsletter. Topica calls them discussion groups, and so does Deja News. Deja News uses a sort of Usenet format to maintain discussion groups.

One of the best ways to start a newsletter is by using a management site, such as Topica. These sites help you organize your mailing list, handle the opt-in/opt-out functions, store your past newsletters, and a great many other valuable services, all for free.

One of the greatest benefits of using Topica is that they will promote your mailing list to their vast network of mailing list subscribers, often cross-promoting into similar genres to pull more signups to your list.

To find out more about how Topica works and to sign up to start your own e-mail list, go to:

http://www.topica.com/

Topica lets you start your own e-mail discussion list or newsletter in just a few quick steps. You can customize how you want your list to work, or just go with the basic default options. And, you can control who joins the list, and invite the people you want.

If you want to use Topica or a similar service to handle people signing up from your own Web site and promotions, simply point them to Topica's sign in page for your list.

Topica also provides some great articles and resources on starting, maintaining, and building your business through newsletters. Here are some resources to check out:

http://www.topica.com/resources/index.html

You can also check out these other list management sites:

Liszt
http://www.liszt.com/
Large searchable directory of 85,000 e-mail lists. You don't use Liszt to read or access e-mail lists. They just help you find lists of interest to you, tell you how to get more information, and how to join.

Topica offers Liszt.Com, the mailing list directory

Listtool.com
http://www.listtool.com/
A service for finding and subscribing to discussion lists. Also provides a good list of resources.

Reference.com http://www.reference.com/
Reference.com has searchable directories of newsgroups and e-mail lists. Over18,000 Usenet newsgroups and hundreds of publicly accessible e-mail lists.

Tile.net
http://tile.net/lists/
This site has pages of the following list categories; Alphabetical listing by description; Alphabetical listing by name; Alphabetical listing by subject; Grouped by host country; and grouped by sponsoring organization.

Publicly Accessible Mailing List
shttp://paml.net/
This is a list of e-mail lists that is posted once each month to the Usenet newsgroups. This Web site maintains an archive of the list that is also searchable.

L-Soft's CataList
http://www.lsoft.com/lists/listref.html
CataList has a database of over 17,000 public LISTSERV lists on the Internet. You can search for e-mail lists of interest, and get information about LISTSERV host sites.

The List of Lists
http://catalog.com/vivian/interest-group-search.html
This site allows you to search one of the largest directories of special interest group e-mail lists available on the Internet. You can also add your own list and find other e-mail list related resources.

ListsNet
http://www.listsnet.com/
ListsNet comprises of a directory of public e-mail lists with features that allow you to browse and search. All the e-mail lists are categorized into a hierarchy making it very easy to drill down into topics and their sub-topics to browse related e-mail lists in focused subject areas.

Using this online live prong also means that you will be going to other music sites similar to your own, and requesting link exchanges. It's a slow, boring job. It gets faster after you've been doing it awhile, but the burn-out factor is high.

But a great deal of the marketing progress happens in link exchanges. By doing the work, you set yourself apart from 95% of the other musicians out there who are too lazy to do it.

Even at this level, you are facing stiff competition, but you are at least in the running. You are taking part in your own success, shaping your own destiny, and doing it yourself.

You can also recruit other members of your group to partake in this activity. Unfortunately, I can tell you that, unless they are really dedicated, they will quickly tire of requesting link exchanges.

The main drawback to having someone help you is that the other person invariably ends up repeating the same steps as you, so a well-defined plan is in order. If your partner is posting to bulletin boards, then bulletin boards should be his department. Keep your responsibilities separate, and make sure that you can check your partner's work. Also, please refer to my section on Time Management and Keeping a Schedule.

Live Streaming

By setting up live appearances on your Web site, using streaming video and audio, you will attract a crowd. A good way to do this is to augment your offline live performances by "webcasting" simultaneously through your Web site.

The technology available to do this is not terribly expensive if you approach it the right way. You can purchase a basic Web camera which comes bundled with broadcast software. Couple that inexpensive camera with an ISP capable of handling basic video, you are well on your way to reaching the world.

A small Webcam can get you connected, but often the picture quality is not the best. If you can possibly afford it, try to go with a more sophisticated camera with several different lenses.

You can always graduate to a larger camera later, once you begin to generate some sales from your efforts. You may also be able to interface an existing video camera to your Web connection.

You can also arrange to do more than one simulcast on other video and audio outlets, such as Internet Radio Stations and other portal sites that may carry your video feed.

Portal Sites

A portal site is defined for our purposes as a popular central site where end users go to download free music and to see what kind of offerings are available from independent groups. Some portal sites have a mixture of both signed and unsigned bands, some popular, some not. Mainly, the purpose of the portal site is to provide a central location and develop popularity.

MP3.com is currently the largest such portal site, and its location and popularity on the digital landscape are second to none. My prediction is that MP3.com will be superceded by other companies, or be bought by one of the major communications giants.

No matter which music portal is on top, be certain that you know which players are in the game. Then you can adjust your marketing efforts accordingly.

The growing number of portal sites gives you more places to announce your music and establish a wider Web presence. You will want to organize portal sites in order of their popularity so that you can prioritize your efforts.

> The idea is to establish a Web page or free download area on the top 10 portal sites, and work those as your main priority. The more new product you can place on these sites, the better.

Keeping up with recording new music, creating new download files, and working the portal sites can easily turn into a full time job. If you are careful with your time management, you can maximize your time and your results.

Payola and Advertising

One aspect of the portal sites, particularly MP3.com, is that artists can pay to advertise on the site itself. This can take the form of banner ads or buying a position on a top 10 list seen on each page.

For instance, MP3.com offers its shameless self-promotion option for artists, whereby they can pay or "payola" for a position on the top ten payola list. This list is displayed on every page on MP3.com for a given period, and the link encourages viewers to download your song. Since MP3.com pays you for each download of your music, this can be an effective way to boost not only your popularity, but to make extra money on downloads.

Banner ads can also be a great way to get the word out, but beware, ads can get expensive. The idea is to find the best value for your money in terms of the price you pay per "impression." A single impression is the presentation of your ad to one viewer. This means that you will be paying every time someone goes to the page your banner appears on, whether they click on your banner or not.

Lesser-known portal sites will charge less for advertising, but you will not get as many impressions. Try to find a portal site that will allow you to purchase advertising per click, rather than impression. If you are paying per click, that means that you are paying for people who have clicked on your ad, so you are paying for people who have actually arrived at your site. This pay-per-click advertising model allows you to pay only for the clicks you get on your banner.

Most of the online world uses the pay-per-impression model when they contract for advertisers. In my opinion, this model is overpriced, and it's a risky proposition at best.

Even if a site does not offer you a per-click deal, approach them with that concept anyway. If the site wants to maximize their ad revenue and make money on their unused space, they will likely work you a per-click deal until they can sell that same ad space by impression.

You might also be able to work a deal with the site whereby they act as a reseller for your CD, and you can cut them in for 50% of the profits in exchange for the ad. This is different from an actual affiliate program, which we will cover in a different section.

Working deals on advertising is largely a matter of establishing contacts and asking for what you want. You will be surprised at the number of sites who will be willing to work with you on barter and special arrangements not available to the general public. But you must ask!

SongSpyder.com

SongSpyder.com is *the* place online for indie musicians to visit for information, support, advice, and to list their original music. It's a music information portal site that offers a unique search utility for finding independent music that is currently online.

SongSpyder.com even offers you your own FREE Web page to list your music, as well as electronic press materials to help you in your promotional efforts and to make your music available for sale.

Take advantage of the resources that SONGSPYDER has to offer, and visit:

http://www.SongSpyder.com

A Music Portal
JIMMY AND DOUG'S FARMCLUB.COM

Jimmy and Doug's Farmclub.com is not a record label, not a TV show, not a Web site; it's a convergence-media music business that happens to have a record label, a TV show and a Web site. Like New York's West Fourth and San Francisco's Haight-Asbury in the '60s and Hollywood's Sunset Strip in the '70s, Jimmy and Doug's Farmclub.com in the '00s is the place musicians and music lovers go to discover anything that has to do with music and music-related pop culture, from the best of the world's unsigned talent to collectibles.

By connecting artists and audiences in this extraordinarily direct way, music fans for the first time also have a true voice in determining which artists are given the opportunity to be heard and realize their dreams. The www.farmclub.com Web site offers unsigned artists the chance to reach a worldwide audience by uploading their music, making it available for downloading and streaming to those in the online community. The most popular of these are then invited to appear on "Farmclub.com," the weekly one-hour USA Network television series (Mondays at 11:00 PM EST/PST), to perform on shows headlined by today's hottest and most cutting edge performers.

Farmclub.com, the online record label, signs, develops and promotes artists discovered through the World Wide Web, as well as traditional A&R sources, and distributes their music via Universal Music Group, the global music leader. In addition, a visit to www.farmclub.com promises the latest singles from Farmclub.com bands, behind-the-scenes access, videos from today's biggest acts, classifieds, message boards and more.

Past and future artists appearing on Farmclub.com, which is hosted by Matt Pinfield and Ali Landry, include: Dr. Dre, Eminem, Beck, Macy Gray, Jay-Z, Limp Bizkit, the historic NWA reunion, Enrique Iglesias, STP, Kid Rock, Smash Mouth, Lil' Kim, Static X, Ozzy Osborne, Groove Armada, Pantera, etc., etc., etc.

Jimmy and Doug's Farmclub.com was created by its CEO, Jimmy Iovine, Co-Chairman of Interscope Geffen A&M, and Doug Morris, Chairman and Chief Executive Officer of Universal Music Group (UMG). Andy Schuon serves as Farmclub.com's President and COO. A subsidiary of Seagram's UMG, the world's leading music company, Farmclub.com was formed in late 1999. The "Farmclub.com" television series premiered January 31, 2000; the Farmclub.com Web site launched February 1, 2000, and the debut album from the Farmclub.com record label's first artist, Sonique, was released February 15, 2000.

5
Prong 2:
Online Media Marketing

Media online are the thousands of newsletters, radio stations, newspapers, and press outlets that publish news about indie artists. By making a newsworthy statement about your group or project in the form of the online press release, you can take advantage of free publicity that can reach literally millions of potential buyers.

Since the press release will be your primary tool for accomplishing this, I will first give you a primer on how to compose the press release. Then I'll provide you with a source list of online media contact lists. You can use those lists to assemble your own list of contacts.

Writing the Press Release

A press release, or publicity release, is a one page, double spaced statement, usually composed in 3 or 4 paragraphs.

It contains an announcement about your group, and should be slanted as a newsworthy item. That is, you send the press release to the publications targeted to your target group. The press release must contain new information of interest to the target group of the publication.

A sample press release can and should be sent as an e-mail, in text or HTML format, and composed as follows:

(Your Contact Info Here)

FOR IMMEDIATE RELEASE:

FOLK SINGER TO RELEASE NEW CD

Singer-songwriter and folk troubadour Mark W. Curran will release his new CD on Friday, January 12, 2002 through his own New Media Digital record label imprint, the label president announced Friday.

The new CD, "Dreaming Of The Gold Rush," contains 12 compositions featuring some of Los Angeles' top session players, and has received critical acclaim both online and off.

"I'm excited about this release," Curran said at a recent press conference at the Hollywood Roosevelt Hotel. "It signifies that folk has found a new resurgence in the online community."

Free downloads of music from the CD will be offered at MP3.com, and at Curran's site, located at: http://www.newmediadigital.com

"30"

The press release should be kept concise, and the release relays the who, what, where, why, and when of the news. Reporters need to know the details when composing their stories, and editors use the information to determine whether they will run your press release or not.

Targeting the press release is an art in itself. You do not want to send the PR to publications whose readers would have no interest in your announcement.

Your must research to locate the publications that serve your market, and pursue those publications regularly. You might want to assemble a list of editors and reporters for your contact list. You should keep careful notes concerning what you have submitted to the list, and when. This information helps when making follow-up calls, as essential part of the process.

A week or so after sending the PR, phone or e-mail, you should contact the recipient, and introduce yourself. Tell the recipient that you are following up to confirm that your release has been received.

Don't call an editor using their 800 number, unless they have given you express permission to do so. It's a matter of etiquette.

Don't be offended if they do not remember who you are. These people receive hundreds of e-mails and phone calls every week, and they are buried in an avalanche of information. Simply remind them, make a notation, and move on to your next contact. By keeping detailed notes on your contacts, you'll have a point of reference when you contact them again with new press releases about your latest news.

Don't be personally insulted if many of the publications, particularly the larger ones, do not publish your news. You are competing in many cases with stories of national interest and major label players.

By taking a unique and interesting approach to your news, you may be able to incite the interest of editors and reporters to publish your news. One such angle is what I call the "David and Goliath" technique. This is where you act as the underdog, a talented artist who has decided to go it alone and compete against the big record labels and beat them at their own game.

You will be using sales figures and careful wording to set yourself in the role of David. You may be able to convey to the readers that your persistence, talent, and determination have resulted in far better sales and recognition than you would have achieved had you been signed to a major label.

There are many creative approaches you can take to making your press releases more interesting. It's often good to create a public interest angle that will result in more publications picking up your story.

Establishing as close a relationship as possible with editors, reporters, and their assistants is also invaluable. You will find that when you take a personal approach with these people, some will take a liking to you and your music. Such people will go to bat for you if you show that you are professional, courteous, and persistent.

Editors and writers often move from one publication to another within their industry. Again, by keeping track in your notes so that you know where the editors are now, you can follow your contacts even when they have moved on to a different place of employment.

Use the following resources while preparing and distributing press releases.

Press Release Writing Tips:

> http://www.pressreleasemedia.com/
>
> http://www.realityconcepts.com/vaper/
>
> http://www.xpresspress.com/PRnotes.html
>
> http://www.infoscavenger.com/prtips.htm

See Appendix 6 for details on writing and distributing a publicity release.

Online Media Contact Sources:

> http://www1.Internetwire.com/iwire/home
>
> http://www.thebroadcastWeb.com/
>
> Music Industry News Network
>
> http://www.mi2n.com/

Online Media Contacts Listed By Region

You can obtain an extensive online list of music publications listed by region by visiting: http://www.yahoo.com. Enter "Online Media Contacts Listed By Region" Which will then give you a breakdown by: Home > News and Media > By Region >

Through the Yahoo interface, you can take each state, section by section, and pick those that appear to be within the same genre as your music announcement. By clicking through to these individual sites and analyzing each site, you can amass valuable, targeted contact information for your database.

Publishing Your Press Release Online

Once you have composed your press release, you should publish it online in at least two places. Start by submitting your press release to http://www.PRWeb.com.

PR Web offers free press release distribution

Next, publish the press release, as is, on your own Web site. You can put up links to it from your Web site, and it makes a valuable source of keywords to help search engines in ranking your site.

You can never have too many pages published on the Web with your name on them. After you have registered one page with a spider-based search, that search engine's robot will spider your directory and find your additional pages at that time. The spider will index those pages accordingly. That is, if you submit the first page of your directory tree, spider-based engines will "spider" the remaining directory files automatically.

Publishing each press release on your Web site is a small step. But this is a step that can pay enormous dividends over time.

Assembling the Electronic Press Kit

An Electronic Press Kit (EPK) is a publicity tool consisting of interviews, visuals and information about an artist, film production, or any project in the public eye. It can be distributed on videotape or online.

It is the electronic version of a print press kit. It should contain information of value to publications and editors interested in doing a story about your group or music. Your online press kit should be available at your Web site, and should contain the following:

1. A bio on you and your group members, along with background on the group.

2. Four to five recent press releases about your group's recent activity.

3. Three to four Web-ready photographs, in both color and black and white.

4. Several MP3 versions of your best songs, or a mixed sampler of your music.

5. A list of places where you are performing, preferably online live.

6. Your Web address, and where your music is available for sale.

7. Your e-mail address, mailing address, phone, and fax.

Assembling the EPK is usually done by a publicist, but if you are going it alone and want to save money, there is no reason why you can't do it yourself.

By making your EPK available from your Web site, you can include the URL in all correspondence with journalists and editors and mention it when making up your industry contact list. It is generally better to refer to the URL and have the journalist visit your Web site if they are interested, rather than e-mailing the file unsolicited.

Editors don't take kindly to being spammed by musicians, especially with 100K files they haven't requested. It can set you off on the wrong foot and ruin a valuable contact forever. Be professional in everything you do, and it will pay off in big dividends.

Electronic Business Cards

The E-card (EBC) is the CD-ROM version of the EPK, and generally contains your group's presentation on a compact disk, or available directly from your Web site. It can contain interviews, reviews, sound bytes, videos, lyric sheets, or any other aspect of your group that shows you in your best light. It is usually presented as a program, which runs a certain number of seconds, and allows the viewer to "sit back and watch and listen" as the disk "pitches" the message. It can be a very effective way to get your message across to the media.

For more information on where to get an EBC done for yourself or for your group, contact Total Planet Interactive, a specialist in the field of interactive media and EBC's. Call 1-805-522-3642 and speak to David Love, the owner of TPI.

Writing Articles for Music Publications

Here is an excellent way to get free exposure to your target group. Write a series of articles or reviews that are of interest to the target group for your music. If you play reggae music, for instance, find popular reggae music sites and publications online, and offer to write an article or monthly column for them reviewing the indie or national reggae scene.

Most publications allow a two or three line blurb at the end of your article for the description of the author. This is the place to plug your group and your Web site.

Some publications may even pay you money, or might do a trade with you for banner space to advertise your CD or Web site. Barter is a great way to go, and is a win-win situation for everyone.

Fans will get to know you through the constant exposure your articles and reviews will bring you, and a percentage of these readers will click to your Web site to learn more about you. This will result in more names for your mailing list, and more sales for you.

Internet Radio Stations

One of the biggest growth areas for online music, Internet radio (IR) stations are proliferating by the hundreds. These are basically online areas where people can go to listen to independent music programming that is not controlled by advertisers and commercial interests.

IR can take on many formats and forms, but essentially any station that plays indie music is a good target for your marketing efforts. Some stations play only certain types of music, so make sure your music is the right fit before e-mailing them or submitting material.

Many online radio stations have an online method set up for you to submit your material, but some do not. You should make an attempt to always make your initial contact through e-mail, if possible. By contacting the radio station via e-mail, you are looking to establish a contact there for your contact list. Your first contact method should be a brief letter of introduction, with links to your Web site for the radio contact to view your online press kit, as well as the listen to a few of your songs.

You should send a follow-up one or two weeks later, thanking them for taking the time to review your materials. At that time, you should ask whether they would be open to having you add them to your contact database and mailing list. By keeping careful notes in your database, you can build a very effective marketing list of online radio stations, and you can continue to market to that list.

Online Radio Station Marketing Methods

Let the station owner know you want to take an active part in promoting your music online, and that you would be willing to offer him content (your music), in exchange for promotional consideration. Direct him to your online EPK to make a further positive impression.

Offer to do live or taped interviews, live audio/video performances, call-in periods, contests, or giveaways. You could even host a segment of the show focused on the genre of your own music. You might even be able to get the station owner to trade you some banner advertising space for your efforts.

Even if you don't get the banner space, by going on a program that has high visibility, you will be getting free exposure, and that is the key to using online media for promotion. Make sure you make it clear to the listeners that your music is for sale, and where they can get it.

Online radio is an excellent way to build a following. It is also a great place to send your ad specialties, like T-shirts, mouse pads, screen savers, and a promo copy of your CD. Your primary objective is getting your name in front of the site owner and keeping it there.

Rating the online stations in order of their importance means getting statistics on the number of hits they are getting from listeners. This is not always simple to do. Unless they have hit counters or published statistics, you may have to rely on popularity lists.

My favorite Internet popularity charts are found at:

http://www.100hot.com/

Here you can check to find out what the most popular Web sites are on any given subject.

You can find the top rated music sites, many of them portals, at:

http://www.100hot.com/directory/arts/music.html

They do not, as of this date, have a top list for online radio stations rated in order of their popularity.

One of the best sources for online radio stations can be found at:

http://wmbr.mit.edu/stations/list.html

This list includes brick and mortar radio stations that have Web sites, as well as streaming radio stations, so it takes a bit of research to find only the stations that feature online radio. However, it is not a bad idea to contact brick and mortar radio stations s well.

Many of these stations are open to receiving indie music, particularly college radio, so do not discount them in your promotions. The fact that you can reach them online qualifies them for your contact list, as long as they feature your genre of music, and are open to receiving materials about new artists online.

A nice list of lists for radio stations is at:

Base For Online Radio Stations

http://www.nanana.com/radiostations.html

Some other cool places to find listings of online radio stations is:

Real Networks
http://realguide.real.com/

Live 365 Radio Revolution
http://www.live365.com/home/index.html

V-Tuner
http://www.vtuner.com/

Internet Radio Lists
http://www.Internetradiolist.com/

Keep in mind, as with all the listings in this book, that new sites are being added daily and old ones going offline.

Online Radio Station Introduction Letter

Your initial contact with an online radio station will likely be through their direct Web site interface, where you will be able to fill out their form and submit your music. However, there will be times when you should make your initial contact through a letter of introduction. This letter can then be e-mailed to the contact listed on the Web site.

A sample letter is as follows:

Mr. Tony Richardson
Director Of Programming
.Com Radio
tony@comradio.com

Dear Mr. Richardson,

I am an independent recording artist seeking exposure on your radio station, and am inquiring into the possibility of submitting some of my music for your review in consideration of netplay.

My music is in the folk-rock vein, an eclectic hybrid of electric folk and americana pop some have likened to the Byrds or Tom Petty and the Heartbreakers.

I invite you to visit my site at: http://www.mysite.com and have a listen to some of my tunes, and even take a look at my press kit.

I believe your listeners will find the music a great addition to your current offerings.

Sincerely,

Mark W. Curran
The Mother Folkers
http://www.mysite.com
me@mysite.com

You may also wish to use the letter format as a follow up to your initial music submission, to remind them of your music, and to gather further information for your contact database. Make sure to allow plenty of time between contacts, as many online radio stations are besieged with submissions. By putting forth a highly professional presentation, your submission will stand out above the rest, and be taken more seriously.

Online Jukeboxes

Some sites are a hybrid of a portal site, online radio station, and or jukebox. Many of the major search engines are creating such areas to promote indie music, and one of the biggest is Yahoo, in partnership with Broadcast.Com. You can check out their indie music portal/online jukebox station at:

http://www.broadcast.com/music/CD_jukebox/

The jukebox is essentially a select and play system, where the online radio station is programmed by an operator who selects the music. The operator places all of the announcements and sometimes commercials during the programming.

Starting Your Own Online Radio Station

If you have a type of music that is not being given enough attention by the more popular online radio stations, you may want to consider starting one yourself. This can be a lot of work, and take up huge amounts of your time, but can pay off in big dividends.

Should you build up a large following to your radio station, you will be in the enviable position of capturing the top advertising spots for your own music, and since you will be selling to a niche targeted group, your sales ratios should be relatively high. As your radio station attracts more listeners, you can also sell ad space to other artists to help increase your revenue.

An additional way to start your own virtual jukebox playlist, is by using MP3.com's interface, available at: http://www.mp3.com.

Radio Broadcast Software

There are a many streaming software solutions and packages that allow you to set up your own net radio broadcasts and I'll list two here.

Shoutcast instructions can be found at the Radiospy site:
http://www.radiospy.com/running.shtml

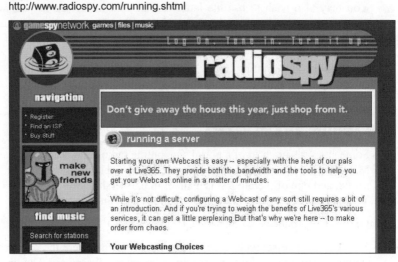

Radio Spy: Start your own webcast and promote it

LiveCast, which is used with the Live365 site is another great software package that can be used in conjunction with an online radio station portal site. LiveCast software allows you to make your own Internet radio broadcasts, mix songs, make announcements, even track your listeners! I have to admit, this one really floored me, particularly the price: it's free!
http://www.live365.com/home/index.html

There are more online radio stations and new broadcast software coming out each month, so keep your eye on our site and also out on the net for updates on this exciting capability.

Microsoft Internet Radio Station

See Appendix 7 for details on the Microsoft Internet Radio Station.

Satellite Radio Stations

The latest installment in the high tech audio revolution is satellite radio. Many of the new cars are being equipped with radio receivers capable of capturing satellite radio signals, and satellite radio broadcasts, or "satcasts," show potential for dominating the current commercial airwaves.

"Satcasting" works the same way as the dish networks you see on home roofs. A small sat dish aimed at a space satellite picks up programming being beamed to the satellite by a central content source. Satcasting will likely be a commercial free, subscription-based entertainment medium, though this may change. Satellite radio has been around for awhile, but it has been only recently seen as a viable alternative to commercial radio, available from every car and home.

The point is, many satellite radio stations will be looking for unique, indie music. By jumping on this new technology at its inception, you may be a step ahead of your fellow indies and capture more market share by getting your music to these outlets first.

The original Public Radio Satellite System was built in 1979 and 1980 with funds provided through the Corporation for Public Broadcasting. The system today transmits over 20,000 hours of programming to more than 400 participating "downlink" radio stations.

One of the most aggressive emerging players in the new commercial-based applications of this technology is XM. This company has closed major financing and has already begun putting its programming infrastructure together. It's partnered with Hughes, CNN, and a number of other high powered players.

XM™ Satellite Radio

Based in Washington, D.C., XM™ Satellite Radio was founded in 1992 as American Mobile Radio Corporation. In 1997, the Company purchased one of only two satellite radio licenses from the FCC to deliver this cutting-edge service. Renamed XM Satellite Radio Inc. in October, 1998, XM Radio has assembled a team of executives from the leading entertainment, telecommunications, consumer electronics, and satellite companies and has attracted the world's leading consumer electronics companies, automotive manufacturers, programming partners, radio talent, and support personnel. In addition, XM Radio has attracted a powerful group of strategic investors—including Motient (formerly American Mobile), General Motors, DIRECTV, Clear Channel Communications—as well as a group of financial investors.

Industry projections on satellite radio have been positive. The New York Times reported in 1999 "We estimate there are 60 million potential subscribers." (August 27, 1999). "Satellite radio is on its way...offering radio its first real competition in 80 years."

(*Billboard*'s Year End Issue 1998)

I expect commercial and corporate interest will come to dominate the satcast field, much as they have the commercial broadcast fields, but with more creative latitude for indie programming. The masses have proven they want to hear indie artists, and the masses will dictate, at least to a certain degree, what kind of programming they want.

My recommendation is to contact every satellite service you can find to inquire about putting your music programming on their transponder. Use the emerging technology of satellite radio as another tool in your arsenal.

Promoting Your Radio Station

Here are 10 ways to promote your online radio station, courtesy of Live365.com:

1. Send radio cards to your friends, family, and mailing list.
2. Put a link to your radio station in your e-mail signature.
3. Rotate your music and change your playlists.
4. Maintain a mailing list.
5. Include a background file about you, the artist on your station.
6. Create broadcasts at different bit-rates.
7. Plaster your radio station URL everywhere, cups, mugs, T-shirts, etc.
8. Be creative in your productions.
9. Visit chat rooms, and announce your station there.
10. Take part in message boards and chat rooms on radio station portals.

Portable Internet Radio

With the emergence of digital wireless technology and handheld computers, it is now possible to receive Webcasts from Internet radio stations on portable handheld devices. This has opened up the possibilities for marketing your music online, because more types of users are now tuning in to these stations due to increased portability.

Portable Internet Radio runs hand in hand with portable MP3 capture and playback devices, allowing users to create their own programs of digital music from their home computers and play them back on small "Walkman"-style devices. By opening up the demand and increasing portability and flexibility of the capture and playback of indie programming, technology is opening the marketing floodgates for the indie artist.

The important thing is to seize the moment now. Start establishing your market share of the listening audience before the field is overrun with competitors and commercial interests.

Here's a guide to the leaders in Internet Radio, courtesy of About.Com:

Kerbango
http://www.kerbango.com
A search engine specifically for audio on the Web, Kerbango is particularly geared toward finding and rating radio station broadcasts.

Passport To Web Radio, Second Edition
John Campbell, Tony Jones
The complete guide to setting up your own Net radio station.
Paperback.

Real.com
http://www.real/com
Real Networks is the developer of the Web's most popular streaming technology.
Realmedia Complete: Streaming Audio and Video over the Web

Webcasters.org
http://www.Webcasters.org
This organization serves as a meeting place for companies interested in the delivery of multimedia audio and video.

Virtual Library: Audio
http://archive.comlab.ox.ac.uk/audio.html
This bare bones site contains a cornucopia of audio resources, including an extensive list of online radio stations.

3WK
http://www.3wk.com
This St. Louis-based Net radio station is a good example of a well run enterprise - a very popular station.

Batanga
http://www.batanga.com
Batanga is available in English and Spanish, and is committed to playing the best in Spanish music.

Billboard Radio
http://www.billboardradio.com
This site is big. It's an online broadcast version of the print magazine Billboard. Good way to keep up with the mainstream of online radio.

Imagine Radio
http://www.imagineradio.com
This hugely popular site enables you to build your own Internet radio station (in other words, create your own playlist.)

MusicMonster
http://www.musicmonster.net/
This station's motto: "Where your music is more than just another link."
MusicMonster is a vehicle for unsigned artists to get their music heard.

National Public Radio
http://www.npr.com
One of the original pioneers in streaming audio broadcast, NPR offers a wealth
of programming.

Pseudo.com
http://www.pseudo.com
Much more than a radio station, Pseudo is streaming media and hip hop
Webcasting at its most hip - this is what the kids are dancing to. Bulletin board
and chat areas.

Rolling Stone Radio
http://www.rollingstone.com/
Broadcast by the well known music magazine, it's currently featuring the DBRN
(the David Bowie Radio Network), along with a large selection of pop, rock,
dance and hip hop music.

Spinner
http://www.spinner.com/
Spinner is one of the Net's biggest radio stations, with everything from country to
jazz to New Age. A well-run site.

Tunes.com
http://www.tunes.com/
This hugely popular site calls itself "The Internet's Music Hub," and generally
lives up to the name. Download MP3s, watch Webcasts, read current news -
Tunes.com is a radio station and more.

World Music Radio
http://worldmusicradio.org/
"The World Is Listening," says this station. And indeed, not only listening, but
contributing. Here you'll hear creative works from musicians all over the globe.

6
Prong 3:
Offline Live Marketing

It is important to recap a point made earlier—in order to have a successful online marketing campaign, you must also work hard to establish your offline marketing efforts. The lifeblood of any performer is performing live, for it is in live performances that the most public awareness is made about the artist.

Live gigs are the only way to really see effective results from your online efforts, particularly at the beginning of your career when you are working to establish a following. In the real world, recording artists must tour constantly to remind the public and to stimulate sales of new product.

While the focus of this book is primarily on marketing yourself online, I am covering some essential aspects of using your live performances to boost your online presence. Some of these have already been covered, such as the placement of your Web site address on everything your band offers to the public.

One element of live performance I consider worth mentioning here, is that it is helpful to find live performance opportunities outside of the mainstream. Bars and clubs are often the worst places for a band to try to sell their music and create an awareness, mainly because these venues are so competitively sought by other groups and artists. Many clubs also require you to play a lot of covers of top 40 and pop, and to have at least four hours of music in your repertoire.

These requirements are at odds with your objective, since you are going to want to record and sell your original recordings, not do covers of someone else's songs. The reasons for this are many. First off, why copy someone else's music, for which you must (technically) pay them a royalty?

And why would someone want to purchase your version of someone else's song? I'm not saying that there is not a market for covers, but the real money is in selling your own songs. Plus, the crowds in clubs are often drinking, and can be quite demanding in their expectations.

You don't need to play four hours of music simply to reach a crowd who is more likely to be concerned with getting drunk or finding a sexual partner than in buying your CD. I don't mean to be down on the club scene, I played them for years and made an excellent living in them, but I learned that playing live for a living and selling your product are two different things.

The idea here is to work smarter, not harder. By focusing your playing efforts on doing shorter performances in non-music settings, you will be gaining a more appreciative audience in much less time. You will also make way more sales.

Not that it's easy money. You've got to get on the phone and arrange these bookings, build a contact list, and follow up. Then you have to travel to these places and set up and break down, not to mention perform, but you'll also have the pleasure of taking money for your CDs, plus selling and signing autographs. When was the last time you were asked to sign an autograph in a club, except for maybe the bar tab?

Jana Stanfield offers some great tips on creating performance opportunities in her book, *The Musician's Guide To Making & Selling Your Own CDs & Cassettes*. I'll share a few of these with you here, along with some insight of my own.

Getting Unconventional Gigs

What you are looking for are pre-assembled audiences, people who are gathered for some other purpose than listening to music. These informal (or formal gatherings) could be banquets, meetings, church groups, political speeches, anywhere people congregate. Even a busy shopping center, marketplace, or shopping mall might be an excellent way to get exposure, provided you have worked out arrangements with the management beforehand.

A perfect example of this type of exposure and marketing can be seen in the grass roots subway musician movement in the underground subway stations of New York City. This kind of playing for spare change might not be your style, but the model it provides is a valuable one. By pre-arranging a free thirty minute concert to an alternative audience such as this, you will find a much more appreciative crowd, and one that is much more apt to buy your product and sign up for your mailing list.

The possibilities for alternative venues for your music are really endless, they exist in every town, every city, no matter how large or small. In fact, the smaller the town, the more appreciative the audience can be.

Jana Stanfield earns well over $30,000 a year playing to banquets, meetings, associations, and church groups. She even plays small house concerts where friends in groups as small as 15 people gather in a living room for a half hour or hour of music!

She started by playing these types of engagements for free, with the caveat that she could make her CDs available for sale. This resulted in a great number of CD sales, a stellar mailing list, and as a result, a large following.

The point of this section is to show you that there are appreciative audiences anywhere two or more people are gathered. You may be surprised at how many of these people will pay you to play, or at least will allow you a half hour of their time to play for free and plug your CD.

If you can sell 15 CDs at every gathering you play to, and you play to 20 such groups per month, you could sell $4500 worth of product per month, part-time. If your cost per unit to manufacture those 300 CDs is $2 each, you've made a profit of $3900! At the same time, you'll be gathering names for your mailing list, and that mailing list does lead to future sales.

Of course, your exact sales will fluctuate, but I want you to see that alternative outlets for your music do exist. You need only take advantage of them. In many cases, clubs and bars are not good places to build a career, to build a following, or to sell product.

Of course, there are exceptions to this rule, depending on the kind of music you play. For example, if you do heavy metal rock, it may be hard to find a good fit in a non-traditional music setting to play your music. You may find that building your following in a club might work best for you.

For singer-songwriters playing in small numbers, such as singles, duos and trios, the alternative method works quite well. To develop your online business and to increase your sales, look for unconventional places where people may be gathered to find an unlimited number of outlets for your music.

7
Prong 4:
Offline Media Marketing

In this technological age, the worlds of online and offline media are blurring. Many brick and mortar media, such as newspapers, magazines and radio stations have established strong online counterparts. By using the online versions of existing media, you can strengthen your marketing results a hundred-fold.

Although our subject remains online marketing, these online versions of traditional offline media can be gold mines in waiting, and cannot be ignored in any discussion of online marketing. The point of selecting the media to be incorporated in your media contact list depends largely upon the audience each publication or media outlet serves.

Daily newspapers, whether they be online or off, usually publish news of local interest to their readers, along with breaking national news, but they also look for human interest stories. The story of your group finding success going up against the big guns of the Big Record Companies (The David and Goliath Method) is one such human-interest angle to use.

Another approach is to attach your musical efforts to a cause of national interest, such as muscular dystrophy, AIDS, or the homeless. Specialized non-profit organizations are always looking for help and volunteers, and they are likely to be receptive to receiving a percentage of your profits. You might consider doing fundraising events for these charities. That could involve doing concerts and other live appearances while donating some or all of the funds to their cause.

By making an arrangement with an important non-profit organization, you help a worthy cause. You also create a story of national interest, because you have affiliated yourself with a high-profile cause. Publications always get behind public service and charitable causes, because that generates goodwill within the communities they serve.

You know well that there are many causes in addition to those mentioned. You'll find an unlimited number of ways to carry out this method. Many of these charities have local, state, and national chapters where you can reach an audience on a scale not possible when maintaining a strictly local focus.

Songwriting for Local, State or National Impact

Another great method for attracting attention to your band or self is to write and record a song about something that is of local, state or national concern that has sparked controversy or great emotion. Perhaps there is landmark in your city in danger of being torn down, or a local resident you would like to honor.

On a national level, you might consider writing a song about a nationally recognized person who died young and tragically. Or you could honor some great achievement by an unknown person who made big news headlines by performing an heroic deed.

You could even write a humorous song about something breaking in the national headlines. These kinds of "novelty" songs not only make great news stories, but they also can be picked up by brick and mortar radio stations for airplay. Monster hits can result. What you are doing is hitching yourself to larger vehicle, and this method of marketing can be extremely effective, yet it is little used.

Media Mailing Lists

Mass mailing to the media is a tricky business, but this is a process that can pay off if you can locate lists that are targeted to your specific niche group. In the case of media contacts, this means locating lists of media that serve your target group. The trick is to find mailing lists that are broken down into sub-categories, such as

Radio Stations > Indepedendent > Heavy Metal

or other variation. The beauty of such a list is that it will often include the media contact. Then you can merge the list with your mailer or promotional efforts, such as building your media contact list.

Finding sources for good, up-to-date mailing lists is never easy, and it's an ongoing challenge. A list that's too old will only hurt your efforts, and an unproven list can be an expensive waste of time. When contacting list brokers, the key questions to ask are:

- How old is the list?
- Does it include the contact name and phone number?
- Can it be merged with your word processor?
- Can you recommend any references of clients that have used this list?

Some brokers will handle both online and offline media. You may also wish to inquire into lists that serve the music consumer directly, as a secondary mailing alternative, such as mailing a flyer describing your latest release. This could be most effective if you can pinpoint your target buyer from previous purchases.

For an example of using a list of your target market, think about a group that plays music of interest to Metallica fans. There exists somewhere a list of consumers who have purchased Metallica's latest release. If you can purchase that list, you might be able to break the list down further into zip codes or local area codes, and do a mailing of 1000-5000 pieces to those targeted consumers.

The hunt for the list will be the hardest part of the equation. Here are three sources for lists:

Abacus
http://www.abacusdirect.com/

Great Lists
http://www.greatlists.com/

Mailing List Brokers List
http://www.nerdworld.com/nw9490.html

8
Your Marketing Plan
Putting It All Together

So far, we have covered a number of online and offline methods to market your music. Here we will recap and add some steps you will need to take in order to implement your marketing plan, putting it all together, and managing your time and resources for optimal efficiency.

Step 1:
Record the product

Record and mix your master CD, then make up two to three short clips for MP3 download/streaming.

Step 2:
Package Your Product

Make up your graphics, songlist, and covers. You can either:

- send the package to a manufacturer for pressing
- make your own limited quantities using your own computer

Step 3:
Prepare Your Marketing Materials

Assemble EPK: Photos, Bios, Backgrounder, EBC.

Step 4:
Build Your Web Site and Get It Hosted

- build Web site or hire Web designer
- contact a hosting company to host site
- maximize meta tags and keywords
- submit site to all major search engines

Step 5:
Organize Contact List System

- use Goldmine or other contact management software
- use 3x5 cards

Step 6:
Start Listing on Portal Sites

At this point, you will go to MP3.com and other portal sites, and establish a Web presence there. You will upload your music files and list your promotional materials, with a link to your Web site. This will be your primary foundation. Bookmark all portal sites and keep them in a linkable file, for fast access.

Step 7:
Begin Online Campaign

- e-mail online radio stations with your letter of introduction
- prepare and send online media press release
- prepare online radio station release
- post first round of Usenet newsgroup releases
- set up live Web appearance date
- start online radio station
- write first newsletter for your first target group
- secure live online radio station interview or tape interview
- begin posting to chat rooms and bulletin boards

Step 8:
Begin Offline Campaign

- set up local record store appearances
- contact indie radio stations, such as colleges
- have promo materials printed, such as bumper stickers, t-shirts, magnetic car signs, window cards, stickers, etc. Begin placing materials and do giveaways.
- set up live appearance schedule, including radio station interviews
- send press releases to all local media, such as newspapers and radio
- assemble postal mailing list and do first mailing to first target group
- contact local office of a national charity and offer to do a live concert in exchange for promotion of your group's Web site and CD
- call your local media and tell them the news you are getting local and national coverage. The publicity machine is a like a snowball, and it feeds on itself.

Step 9:
Repeat

Repeat the above steps, again and again!

Remember, once you have your program in place, much of marketing is persistence, repetition, and follow-up to your previous cycle of work. As each new event occurs with your group, you will be making yet another round of submissions. These submissions will inform all your online and offline media of your latest exploits or success. The submissions will be in the form of press releases, live announcements, and media events such as a listening party to kick off your new CD or even the completion of your new song!

Marketing is really all about information flow, the creation of information, the exchange of information, the delivery and follow up:

Create news story > write up press release > distribute press release > follow up

Although the news will change, the process by which the news gets delivered stays the same. As you establish new channels of distribution, the process widens. Generally, you are contacting your contact list, sending and following up on e-mails regarding your band's latest news, releases, concerts, songs, plans, etc.

Yes, it's a constant time-consuming, challenging job, but someone has to do it. After you do it for awhile, the glamour fades, and it can become monotonous. It's hard for one person to do it all.

In the hierarchy of traditional music business marketing, many of these departments are handled by specific agencies. Sometimes it's the record company, the concert promoter, the song plugger, the retail store, but always, the job remains the same:

To get your product before potential buyers

As an independent, unless you can afford the luxury of hiring specialists for each job, you must do the jobs yourself. There is no other way, because if you ignore the area of marketing and exposure, if you don't produce good publicity and follow up, you will find your career dead in the water.

Marketing is about making one helluva racket, and making sure the right people hear it. If you have to be obnoxious, abrasive, incorrigible, and just plain stubborn, be that way. It is better to make a commotion than to stay silent in quiet pride, humbly bowing to the idea that by keeping your mouth shut you and your music will miraculously rise from obscurity into the mainstream. The only thing silence and pride will buy you is more obscurity.

You've got to become a one-man or one-band promotional machine, willing to do anything and everything it takes to get your music in front of the people who are most likely to buy it. The only cardinal rule here is — don't alienate or insult your buyers. Deliver a consistent image.

If your personality is unsuited to the task, then hire someone who will do the marketing for you so that you can move on with the business of making music.

The best bit of advice I ever heard on marketing was this:

"Good marketing done inconsistently is not nearly as effective as bad marketing done consistently. But the only way to true success is to do good marketing, consistently. "
Time Management

Our only true asset is time, yet we often take time for granted. Many people accustomed to working for someone else may not possess the discipline required to work long hours on their own. For these people, hiring others to do the job may be the only way.

But for those who must do it themselves, there are other pitfalls. You may have the drive, but do not have the ability to prioritize tasks and maximize allotted hours to getting the work done. Sitting alone at the computer, you may find your attention turning to other distractions, and there are endless distractions online. Add to the online distractions the offline distractions like ringing phones, unannounced visitors, screaming kids, a lonely spouse, the list goes on and on.

The only way to overcome this difficulty is to set up a priority list and a work schedule, and stick to it, every working day. Since you are also a musician, you will need to work your playing, practice, and recording time into your weekly schedule.

It is important to have a workspace where you can be alone, free of distractions. If you work from home, that might mean setting up a small workspace in the garage or attic, or in a room isolated from the rest of the house. A phone line for the computer and a phone line with a phone that remains switched off while you do your work may be the only way to have uninterrupted time. In fact, some find that renting office space outside the home is the only way to get free of the temptation to become sidetracked from the task at hand.

The real trick to marketing is doing it in an intelligent, focused, and consistent manner. By consistent, I mean every working day. You need to manage your time, and the best way to do it is on a schedule sheet. Here is an example of one of my daily schedule sheets:

Monday:

6:00am	Power up computer - check e-mail - have coffee - check phone messages
6:45am	Post to newsgroups 1-25
8:00am	Write press release for new CD - submit to media list #3
9:30am	Breakfast
10:00am	Link exchanges
11:00am	Search engine submissions
12:00pm	Return phone calls
1:00 pm	Lunch Break - run errands, drop off dry cleaning, go to bank. (Gym on Tues, Thurs.)
2:00pm	Return to office - check phone and e-mail messages, return calls
2:30pm	Cold call offline and online radio stations about new promo
3:30pm	Follow up with existing radio stations on last week's press release
4:30pm	Mail online press kits to Folker, WPPR, and Web TV
5:00pm	Finish outstanding work, make up schedule for tomorrow
6:00pm	Power down computer and leave office

Each day as you finish the day's activities, you may be jotting down notes for the next day's schedule. Then at the end of each working day, you will make up your next day's schedule.

Keeping organized like this, you will develop a priority list that will maximize your time and effectiveness, providing a clear and consistent marketing plan for moving ahead at full steam. When you replicate this kind of focused effort over time, you will begin to see very rewarding results.

For an excellent resource in time management, I recommend the following book: *The One Minute Manager*, by Ken Blanchard, co-authored with Spencer Johnson

It's extremely important to keep proper nutrition, exercise, and rest a part of your daily routine. The body and mind are complex machines that require the right maintenance. If you take care of the basics, your performance in all areas of your business will operate at peak efficiency.

First you need proper nutrition, adequate sleep, and an exercise regimen such as walking, going to the gym, or weight lifting. Second, you should take frequent breaks from the computer to stretch, drink lots of water, and keep the body fueled and nourished.

Eyestrain is a constant problem for computer professionals. Relaxing the eyes on a regular basis to avoid eyestrain is important. Look away from the computer every twenty minutes or so, focus on far away objects, blink the eyes for moisture, and try to rest them every hour. I lie down and place headphones on my ears, playing meditation music. I also put a cool compress over my eyes, like a cool, moist washcloth I keep in the fridge.

Taking frequent breaks to relax the eyes and mind will give you more strength to carry on over the long haul, and save wear and tear on your eyes and mental state.

Short Term vs. Long Term Results

Many people operate under the popular misconception that the Internet brings instant sales results. Of course, in some respects, that's true. A measurable response is often quicker on the net because people can respond more quickly to your promotions. But this is where any resemblance to a quick profit ends.

Most of the clients I have worked with are often disappointed when results do not come in a matter of weeks. For those who are doing their own marketing, the lack of immediate response is one of the biggest reasons why they give up too soon.

You must view your online marketing as a long-term investment strategy, one that will pay dividends over time. It is not the route to short-term, windfall profits.

Think of marketing on the Internet as the sowing of seeds. It takes time to till the soil, plant the seeds, move on down the line, nurture the seedlings as they grow. Over the days and weeks, with the right climate and water, those seeds will begin to sprout, imperceptibly at first.

As the weeks stretch into months, you will see the makings of a decent crop, a cash crop, if you will, that will continue to yield results for you the year round. But not all seeds grow, and not all trees yield fruit.

In this modern age, we are accustomed to getting the things we want right away. But things of the greatest value are often the most difficult to obtain. In order for good marketing to be effective, we must carry out the marketing consistently over time.

The man searching for short-term profit may want to take up day trading or short-term stock speculation for an investment vehicle. The Internet is no place for short-term thinking.

If there is one solid lesson to remember in this entire book, it's the fact that building a successful business takes time and considerable sacrifice. The relative ease and inexpensive access that the Internet affords brings us an abundance of buyers, but it also brings us a surfeit of competitors.

It's rather easy to throw up a Web site using a template, and it's easy to host the site with a budget host, and it's easy to call the site a business. The reality of actually building a money-making business on the Web takes a great deal more work.

The musician seeking to build his fortune online must do so with a great deal of forward thinking. It will require a lot of fortitude and wisdom, confidence to know the labor will result in profit, and above all, the patience to persevere through the rough times that will surely occur at the inception of any new business.

The number one reason why new online businesses fail is because the owner of the business hoped to make a quick fortune without effort, knowledge, or patience. There is nothing wrong with dreaming of instant wealth, as long as the dreamer knows that it is inherent in our nature to dream of gold without digging, but there comes a time when the fantasy must end and the work must begin.

I have worked with many people in the music and Internet marketing business. One characteristic I've noticed in common among those who succeeded was the willingness to do whatever it took to make their dreams happen. Success rarely requires talent or intelligence. Rather, it's the persistence of working at the business every day, chipping away at the goal week in, week out, that makes the difference.

I'm sure you've met virtuoso players who played so well that you at first wondered why they were not playing music in the big leagues. But then, when you got to know the person, you found they had problems getting along with other players, or ego difficulties, or a drug or alcohol challenge, or any of a thousand other limitations. The most common problem is laziness, the unwillingness to do what it takes to make the dream happen.

Work your marketing plan, work it hard, every day. Avoid short-term thinking, and keep your eye on long-term results. This is what separates the successful players from the rest of the pack, and it's what will make you the rising star that shines above the rest.

9
Affiliate Programs and Sales Partners

The following two Internet marketing methods can be crucial to your marketing effort. They boost your sales considerably, and every musician should use these methods in getting their music to the largest possible audience.

Affiliate programs

Broadly defined, an affiliate program allows you to sign up other Webmasters to act as sales agents who list your advertising for a percentage of the sale. In many respects, these Webmasters become sales agents for you, agents who are working on a commission basis. I prefer to call these associates "sales affiliates."

Sales partners

A sales partner, for the sake of this discussion, is defined as a large, established online retailer who advertises your product for a commission. You join their affiliate program, and become an affiliate for them, not the other way around.

Both of these methods are almost identical in structure, but in scope, they are quite different.

How Affiliate and Sales Partner Programs Work

They go by many names: associate programs, affiliate programs, or referral programs. All of these mean pretty much the same thing—you help a company promote their products or services and generate sales, and in return they pay you something. They generally give you a special URL with a code embedded in it in order to track sales from your Web site.

Some of the better known referral programs for selling music online are Amazon, Barnes and Noble, Music Boulevard, CDNow, and Yahoo. These companies offer tremendous opportunities for the seller of indie music, for these entities have a lot of traffic and potential buyers. Their great power to attract sales is enhanced by their search capabilities, whereby a Websurfer can find almost anything they are looking for in a short amount of time.

Amazon.Com's Online Retailing Program

Add to the list above the great auction sites, such as EBay, Half.com, Yahoo, and Amazon. On those sites you have powerful sales tools that are virtually free to use.

Setting up Your Own Affiliate Program

There are many ways to set up your own affiliate program. They vary mostly in the amount of autonomy you demand.

Adding Affiliate Program Software to Your Site

You can set up your own program by purchasing special affiliate program software to interface with your merchant account for seamless sales tracking and online commerce. If you are running your own program, you will be responsible for handling the payout of commission checks to your affiliates. Be aware that managing payout can become a time consuming task.

Setting an affiliate program up yourself generally runs about $1000, after all the technical and setup work is completed. You can do that work yourself if you are good at programming on the server level. Affiliate program software, which is designed to work as a plug-in to your existing online billing and e-commerce system, can be obtained for between $200-$400.

Using an Affiliate Program Service on Your Site

Some online billing companies offer automatic affiliate program services, such as CCBill, who will manage your affiliate program for you for a percentage of the sale. The advantage to this is that it's a turnkey solution. Within a day you can be processing transactions through your affiliate network. You might consider it a disadvantage that you must pay for the service, but in my opinion, it's worth every penny.

Join an Existing Affiliate Program as a Vendor

There are now several companies that allow you set up a number of existing affiliate programs on your Web site, one of which is called Commission Junction.

Commission Junction is creating a world where people can buy anything, anywhere, anytime as they pursue information and entertainment that interests them. With Commission Junction you join a powerful alliance of online "merchants" that sell products and services on popular "affiliate" Web sites that generate traffic for them.

The results are increased exposure and sales for merchants and commissions for their partner affiliates. Online merchants can increase sales by 15% to 40% or more while creating a whole new revenue stream for their affiliate content sites.

Who is Commission Junction?

Commission Junction is the e-commerce network that enables consumers to buy anything, anytime, anywhere while pursuing information and entertainment that interests them. With Commission Junction, online merchants place their products and advertisements on hundreds of thousands of affiliate content sites all across the Web, creating a virtual sales force that earns commissions for real performance and real sales. These affiliate content sites earn revenues by offering their visitors multiple buying opportunities in and around their content earning a commission on every merchant sale or referral they generate.

Why should I join?

With over two million merchant and affiliate partnerships in the Commission Junction network, our members can significantly increase their revenues, while providing convenient and secure online shopping to their visitors. Commission Junction manages these partnerships through an easy-to-use Web-based interface that tracks every sale and referral, reports all transactions online in real time, and pays each affiliate their commissions in one consolidated monthly check.

How does it work?

Online merchants upload their advertisement banners, buttons and product links to the network, select affiliates to join their program and provide links for placement on their affiliate sites. Merchants can choose to pay their affiliates per click, per referral back to their Web site, or per sale of their products or services. With Commission Junction, merchants have a virtual sales force of hundreds of thousands of affiliates all over the Web, taking their products to consumers, instead of waiting for consumers to come to them.

Affiliate content sites join Commission Junction for free. As a network member, they select from hundreds of prescreened online merchants and sign up those with products that would be of interest to their visitors. Affiliates then place each chosen merchant's banners, buttons and product links within and around the content on their Web sites. Every time one of their visitors clicks on a merchant's link and is referred to the merchant's site or makes a purchase, the affiliate earns a commission.

Commission Junction provides:

- A Web-based service that requires no software installation or upgrades

- Dedicated account managers and a responsive help desk to provide ongoing support

- Reliable and scaleable tracking technology to measure advertising effectiveness

- Real-time reporting that can be accessed with one I.D. and password

- Easy management of affiliate relationships with multiple merchants through one account

- Free payment processing and consolidation of commissions to affiliates each month

- Quick set up for both affiliates and merchants

- Sophisticated fraud management to ensure member security

- Continuous monitoring by an independent third-party provider

Commission Junction is easy to join, easy to use, and it pays for itself. So, join Commission Junction today and generate more revenues by selling everywhere and selling often.

For more information on commission junction, go to:

http://www.MusicMarketingCo.Com

Selling Your Product through Online Retailers

There are major online retailers, such as Amazon.com, Yahoo, and Barnes and Noble, who market and sell your product in exchange for a percentage of the sale. The major retailers require your product, in this case, your compact disk, to be properly packaged and bar-coded. This enables the retailers to track inventory and payout information quickly, and to deliver a professional looking product to the consumer.

To work with the major online retailers, first you sign up with one of these companies and have sent them your sample product. After your product has been accepted, you will be asked to ship a certain number of units to their warehouse for stocking. As those units are sold, you will be sent an automated restocking request.

Often, the terms of payment are "Net 30" days. This means that the retailer pays you within thirty days of your shipment, so you will be out of pocket on your stock for at least one month. However, the good news is that these retailers will generally request only 10 units at a time, unless your product is flying off the virtual shelves.

Much of the time, the price the retailer will pay you will not be based on a commission. Rather, the retailer will pay a price per unit based on the retail price. When you sell your product to a larger distributor who then sells directly to the consumer, you will often be giving deep discounts as high as 60% off the retail price.

The advantage to losing up to 60% of your profit is the volume at which these retailers can move your product. You will have to weigh the advantages and the disadvantages of using these retail outlets in terms of profit over time. Consider your costs and the discounts you are allowing. That is, when you are retailing at $18 per unit, and giving a wholesaler 50% discount, and your price per unit (studio time + manufacturing) and shipping is $3, you've made a profit of $6 per unit.

If you moved 3000 units through wholesalers, that would be a profit of $18,000. That's not bad, especially if the product is moved in fairly short order, which would allow you the funds to have another manufacturing run if the product is in demand.

Attracting Affiliates

Once you have your own affiliate program set up, it's time to visit as many Web sites as possible that feature indie music. You will be looking for sites that cater to the same musical tastes as your target market. You will then seek the e-mail address of the Webmaster, and send him an e-mail requesting he consider your affiliate program for his site. Be sure to point out the benefits of your affiliate program over others. Make your presentation appealing. After all, this Webmaster may be getting many such requests, some of them from larger retailers and wholesalers.

The average commission can range anywhere from 10%-60%. You can adjust your commission payout according to demand, but watch your costs, prices and discounts. Don't price your product too low and your commission structure too high, or you will be breaking even or losing money.

Never underestimate the power of a good affiliate program. It can free up your time from direct selling. An affiliate program can give you enough time to concentrate on administrating your affiliate sales program, attracting more affiliates/salespeople to your door.

The advantage and earning potential of having commissioned salespeople working on your behalf is not lost on many major sales organizations, who know that the power of sales is in the numbers. The more worker bees you have in your hive, the more honey you will generate.

For more information on selling through the majors, contact:

Yahoo Online Merchandising
http://store.yahoo.com/

Barnes and Noble
http://www.barnesandnoble.com/

Amazon Advantage
http://www.amazon.com/exec/obidos/subst/misc/sell-items.html

CDNow
http://www.CDnow.com/

Online Auctions

Another unusual way to market your music online is at the various auction sites. Of course, E-bay is the largest, but there are also hundreds more. Why would anyone want to purchase a CD or tape nobody ever heard of?

The answer to this question is one word, and that word is "collectible."

Your work is a limited edition, a collector's item to those who value the collection of music in the genre you cater to. And although you will likely not generate a great number of sales, people do find auctions to be an additional tool in their online arsenal.

The secret to success with online auctions is the description of your CD or group merchandise. (You can also market T-shirts, videos, photo clocks, or any other merchandise with your group's info prominently displayed.)

When I market my own CD, I list it as:

> *Folk-Rock Music Collectible - Autographed limited edition release of "Dreaming Of The Goldrush," beautifully illustrated and recorded, this 12 song CD by singer-songwriter Mark W. Curran is destined to become a classic. If you like Bob Dylan and America, you will love this CD. Still shrink-wrapped and in mint cond. Bidding starts at $9.*

Now, again, you are not going to be moving a great number of units through auctions, but it is a route you should not ignore. Using the power of words you can describe your item as being a one-of-a-kind and unique collectible destined to increase in value.

10
Hiring a Publicist, Promoter, or Consultant

We can make a strong case for hiring outside services to perform the jobs you do not have the time or capacity to do yourself. Many musicians would prefer to spend their time writing, performing, and creating, and do not wish to be saddled to the desk. This is understandable, and in situations where the budget allows, the hiring of a consultant might be in order. The consultant can help you to determine the best course of action for your particular product.

A good consultant can save you from making costly mistakes and can justify the added expense of his invoice. A consultant will get an overview of your product and objectives and outline some steps for you to take in terms of direction and marketing. He may advise you to hire a publicist, a marketing specialist, or a promoter to help get your music in front of the masses, whether it be online, offline, or both.

Some firms provide many services under one roof, acting as a one-stop shop where you can get all of the services in a more efficient and cost effective way. One such firm is The Music Consultants Company. For an overview of their services, go to:

http://www.musicmarketingco.com

For a listing of such firms, check the search engines under "Music Marketing Consultants," or similar search terms. Online music marketing services is a relatively new field, but a rapidly emerging one, and more entries are sure to proliferate. You may also want to check the classifieds sections of major music publications such as *Cashbox*, *Music Row*, and *Billboard*.

Music marketing firms like to work with artists who have a budget allocated for promotion and marketing. Marketing is a lot like advertising. It can be expensive but it's essential to success. Without marketing, the indie artist cannot expect to realistically achieve good results.

There may be a few firms willing to work for a commission of sales, but this is exceedingly rare. This would be like asking a major magazine to exchange advertising space for a percentage of sales. That doesn't happen very often.

Much like advertising, you must pay for the services of a promoter to get your product out to the people. Then you hope that the people will buy. It is a gamble, an investment in the stock market of public taste. Your product may fly, or it may not. That is the nature of all new business and new brands in the marketplace.

Long-term thinking is vital to your success, for a short-term marketing and advertising program is a waste of money. If you are not in it for the long haul, you might as well put your efforts into something else.

In the advertising world, good product marketers know that repetition yields the best results. It is often said that a person needs to see a sales message on an average of eight times before deciding to purchase. Music marketing is no different.

Also remember that a marketing strategist's primary job is to get an effective sales message out to as many people in your target group as possible. His job is not to directly sell your product, but to provide the impetus for sales. In the end, the product will sink or swim based on its own merits.

It is possible you could spend a great deal of money paying others to market your product, only to find that the product does not sell. Every person entering the marketplace with a new product faces this risk. Even a feasibility study does not guarantee results. In life, as well as in business, there are no guarantees.

However, if you have calculated that you have a good product and can reach your target market, and are in it for the long haul, you have a reasonably good chance for success. You calculate your risks, invest time and money into your product, and promote it accordingly. Going through this process is the only way to really know if your music will appeal to the masses in your target group.

Put it out there! It is the only way to know for sure.

When hiring an outside firm, make sure you get details on the exact services they will provide for you. Likewise, determine the exact cost. An itemized list can help, as well as a breakdown of the frequency of the service.

11
Using Merchandising for Increased Profit

Your music has a built-in product extension, and that product extension is called an ancillary market. The process is called merchandising your group image or name. You see this type of merchandise on sale at concerts, where tables are set up to sell the group clothing, apparel accessories, bumper stickers, posters, and just about anything else you can think of emblazoned with the group's logo or likeness. This type of merchandise can add up to big dollars, and has a very special marketing function. The person wearing it provides you with free advertising and exposure.

In the beginning, an unknown group will find it hard to sell quantities of these items, but as giveaways they make a great promotional tool. As you become more popular, these items can be placed for sale as ancillary merchandise at your concerts and any other promotion you wish to dream up.

Online, your merchandise can find a life of its own. By setting up a small store on your Web site, you can make additional sales on t-shirts, photo clocks, posters, and computer-related items. Merchandising sales can be a significant source of income over time. The right design can create a great demand for the product, even if you are unknown.

Mugs

11 and 15 ounce, dishwasher safe ceramic coffee mugs.

$12.99 each
11 ounce

$14.99 each
15 ounce

Click for view:
🔍 Zoom In On Picture

Get the popular hot mug and wake up with some Faith!

Click for view:
🔍 Zoom In On Picture

See the larger than life action shot of Faith and Funky Gypsy. Wake up!

Artists can sell merchandise imprinted with their promo art

You might even consider giving merchandise away as a way to sell your CD!

A great incentive to making an album sale is to offer something for free. You can have mouse pads, screensavers, T-shirts, just about anything made up with your photo and name on it. Offer one of these items for free if an order is placed for your CD. People love free stuff, and people with marketing savvy use that to great advantage. The principal rule of thumb in merchandising and giveaways is to always include your URL on all your printed items.

When does an advertising specialty, such as a mouse pad, cease to become a give-away? When you are big enough to develop a demand for these same novelties from your core target audience, and they are willing to pay for them.

Merchandise and giveaways can provide you with considerable exposure, and can motivate people who see your name offline to visit your site online. These visits can lead to more hits, more fans, and more sales. Subsequently, these visits lead to more giveaways and more exposure.

What can you imprint? Just about anything. Apparel - Bags - Calendars - Desk Items - Engraved Gifts - Hats - Jackets - Key Chains - License Plates - Lighters - Magnets - Mugs - Pens - T-Shirts - Watches

Those are just a few of the more commonly used items. But what about getting really imaginative with promotion? Here are a few more items that we've found can be imprinted successfully:

Address Books
Aprons
Awards
Badges & Buttons
Balloons
Balls
Banners
Baseball Caps
Binders
Binoculars
Blinking Buttons
Bookmarks
Bottle openers
Briefcases
Business Card Holder
Calculators
Calendars
Cameras
Candles
Can Caps
Candy
CD Player
Cell Phone Caddies
Cigar
Clips
Clocks
Clothing
Coasters
Coin Banks
Computer Accessories
Cookies
Coolers
Crystal
Cups
Embedments
Emergency Flares
First Aid Kits
Flashlights
Flying Disks
Games
Gavels
Globes
Golf Accessories
Golf ball

Golf Shirts
Gourmet Food Items
Guest Amenities
Gum
Gym Bags
Holograms
Ice Scrapers
Jackets
Jet Sketch
Kaleidoscopes
Key Chains
Lanyards
Lap Throws
Lapel Pins
Letter Openers
Lip Balm
Luggage Tags
Magnets
Magnifying Glasses
Medals
Memo Pads
Mending/Sewing Kit
Mouse Pads
Mugs
Napkins
Note Pads
Ornaments
Paperweights
Passport Wallets
Pen & Pencil Sets
Pencil Cups
Pennants
Pens
Personal Alarms
Personal Planners
Phone Calling Cards
Phone Cord Untangler
Plants
Plaques Playing Cards
Plush Toys
Portfolios
Post-it Notes
Puzzles
Radios

Rain Hats
Robes (plush terry)
Rulers
Safety Items
Sandals for the Beach
Screen Dusters
Seat Cushions
Shirts
Signs
Snacks
Softballs
Sports Bottles
Springy Thing
Squeeze Balls
Stadium Cushions
Staplers
Stationery
Steins
Streamers
Stress Balls
Stuffed Animals
Sunglasses
Suntan Lotion
Sweat Bands (head/wrist)
Sweat Shirts
Sweaters
Toiletries
Tool Kits
Tote Bags
Toys
Travel Accessories
Travel Mugs
Trophies
T-Shirts
Tire gauges
Umbrellas
Uniforms
Visors
Watches
Water
Windbreakers
Zipper Pullers
.....and LOTS more!

For more information and prices on specialty imprinted merchandise, visit:

Advertising Specialties Associates
Terry Roberts, Owner
Toll-free: +1 (800) 956-9992
http://www.promoideas.com/

or

Imprint Promotions
http://www.imprint-promotions.com/

12
Setting Up Your Own Internet Record Label

There are thousands of indie artists out there looking to sign with a label. If the majors don't come knockin', they are willing to settle for any label at all that will get them some exposure and some sales.

By starting your own record label, you can become the entity that signs groups and promotes their music, usually for a percentage of the sale. This normally requires a substantial investment of time and money up front, for you will be packaging the product and putting it out there with no way of knowing if it will sell.

There are many ways to cut corners on releasing product from outside groups on your own label. The most obvious way is to do it exclusively online so that you do not manufacture any quantities of product unless the demand calls for it.

If you were resourceful, you could locate groups that have a master already recorded. Then you could promote their CD online for them, through Internet channels, radio stations, links, etc., and never incur a single expense other than your time. If you were selling the product by download only, you would not even incur manufacturing or postage costs.

Now, while all this sounds very appealing, the person going into such a business should proceed with caution. Even if you have successfully promoted your own music this way, you do not necessarily have the capacity to promote the music of others. Promotion requires many long hours of hard work to achieve success.

You will be online and on the net-phone constantly, hustling like there's no tomorrow. Remember, if you are working on commission, making sales will be the only way you eat. And, as the old Italian saying goes, "No sale means no eat!"

But for some, the idea of starting their own online record label has an appeal that cannot be ignored. A record label affords the music impresario a prestige vantage point, a way to get talent to come to him, while commanding a higher level of respect from his industry peers. When you have a label, more doors may open to you, and those doors may lead to some pretty lofty heights.

But once the glamour of the idea fades, keep in mind that it may end up with only you sitting in your dark bedroom for hours and days at a time, trying to plug the music of a group nobody has ever heard of. It can be lonely, devastating work. But the rewards can be great.

There will never be a shortage of new talent looking for a label, and large record companies are always on the lookout for hungry young upstarts with promise. Should you develop a label with a small roster of indie artists and you are garnering some sales and attention, don't be surprised if you are contacted by brokers, looking to buy you out. Mergers and acquisitions are common trends in the music businesses, and small labels are prime targets for buyouts.

When the brokers come calling, you may be able to secure a distribution deal with a major label or Internet label. Such a distribution deal would allow you to focus on getting new artists and recording new product.

Each label handles a specific genre or type of music. If you specialize in Latin dance music, you will be looking to sign groups and artists with a new or interesting spin on that genre. Keep the label specific to that one type of music. If you want to bring out a second genre, go ahead and form another label.

What a Label Does

The record label is responsible for manufacturing and packaging the end product, making sure that such things as bar codes and shrink wrap are correct and that all the elements of getting the disk to the marketplace are handled properly.

A label can also become involved in distribution. Until recently distribution was done only through traditional distribution systems. If your idea of direct distribution is at all appealing to your artists, you may find yourself competing with your own artists for distribution.

A new way to approach the "D" problem is to market your artists' work online, and bypass the brick and mortar system. For online distribution, you will set up a Web site for your label. You will feature your artists under your label/Web site banner, and you will sell their music directly through the Web site. You can also set up a special sub-directory for each artist's own Web site area, accessible through your domain.

No matter how you approach it, the label is responsible for the collection and distribution of sales revenue, so if you are going to become a label, you must understand that bookkeeping is an essential element in your responsibility to your artists. This means keeping track of sales and cutting checks on a monthly basis. For many people, this is a task best left to accountants.

But accountants cost money, so beware when you are enticed by the glamorous idea of starting a record label. The price to pay for this position is measured in dollars and hours.

On the up side, being a label means you call the shots, and you can command powerful respect if you have a label that is getting lots of attention from the fan bases of its artists. From a purely business point of view, labels of all sizes make great takeover targets by larger industry labels and distribution arms.

In the emerging Internet business world, your label can also be an attractive vehicle for new media entertainment companies. New media companies may see profit potential in buying your label and its stable of artists for further exploitation and packaging.

Here is where the odd bedfellows of art and commerce often clash. You may find yourself in the unsavory position of being the bad guy, selling out to the system. The company buying you out may not have your artist's best interests at heart. That is, the buyer may end up giving some of the artists less than favorable account servicing, leaving them to *rot on the vine*. How far your responsibility extends to your artists is a matter of personal and business ethics.

A possible positive aspect of a buyout is that a larger company buying your label may give the label new life, providing your artists with better exposure, distribution, and clout in the marketplace. A buyout for your label can have both positive and negative aspects for the label and for the artists. You must be sure to look at both sides of the coin as you plan your record label strategy.

Essentially, the main steps to setting up your own Internet record label are:

1. Register your domain name.
2. File fictitious name.
3. Open checking account
4. Build Web site.
5. Promote Web site.
6. Actively pursue artists.
7. Release first CD.
8. Promote that CD.

Steps 5-8 will be repeated over and over again with each new artist you sign, and with each subsequent CD they release.

13
Interviews
With Successful Web Artists

Richard Jones

http://www.transoceanic.com

Richard Jones is the founder and leader of the successful group, Transoceanic, which had three songs in the MP3.com top ten concurrently, including the #2 and the #3 positions. They were also the number 4 top earning artists on MP3.com in July 2000, out of 100,000 artists.

How many hours per day do you spend marketing your music online?

Music is currently a part time activity for me, and I have to fit it in around my "day job." So, I get to spend perhaps an hour a day at online marketing. So it is important to get the maximum effect out of each hour.

Can you offer any advice, tips, or tricks to new musicians just starting out in marketing their music online?

The most important thing of all is to realize that the Internet is not in itself a magic source of exposure and money. There are literally hundreds of thousands of other artists out there in cyberspace trying to earn the same dollars that you're trying to earn. So Lesson One (!) is that you must appreciate that promotion is necessary.

Lesson Two is to understand the historical significance of Lesson One. In the past you couldn't market your own music because all of the available channels were controlled by the recording and publishing companies. If you weren't already a success, you couldn't get signed. Now the Internet has put the ability to market your music firmly in your own hands. Although that is a step forward, it does mean work!

Lesson Three is to look for methods of promotion which have a long lasting effect. Too many musicians I see on MP3.com seem to spend much of their time swapping downloads with other musicians.

While there is a place for that if you're just starting and you want to get yourself heard for the first time, the problem with it is that it is completely temporary.

The next day - that person you swapped with is not going to download your music again unless you also download his music again. You're back to first base. So, find things that last. For example, if you can convince a conventional or Web-based radio station to add you to their playlist, that might have a longer term payoff, since you might be on that playlist for a long time.

Lesson Four is to observe and understand the system you're working with. If you're on, say MP3.com - look around, see who's doing well, and how they're doing it. Try to understand what gets you up the charts - is it sales of CDs, or downloads, or simply people visiting your page? If you know what the system is, you can find the most effective ways of promoting yourself.

Finally, find out who's in control - is there someone who can get you a featured artist slot on the site?

Is there any type of music you think does particularly well compared to other types when marketing it online - country, rock, folk, new age, etc.?

I think the amazing thing about the Web is that every type of music has a market - because the audience is so big. However, one notable fact is that there are lots of folks using the Internet at work, with fast connections.

So, music that people want to listen to while at work is probably more popular that you would expect. New age, mood music, relaxation music, that sort of thing. Because of this, for example, we find that we get far more listeners during the week than on the weekend, which surprised us initially.

And this ties up very nicely with our upcoming strategic tie up with a Web-based "health spa".

What accomplishments are you especially proud of with regard to your online success?

Well, it's improving all the time, but here are some accomplishments we're proud of:

- we had three songs in the MP3.com top ten at the same time, including the #2 and the #3 (there are over 500,000 songs on MP3.com);
- we were number 4 top earning artists on MP3.com in July 2000, out of 100,000 artists;
- we now have more than 50,000 listeners per month;

- our total number of listeners is approaching 250,000;
- we are selling CDs all over the world;
- we're featured on over 170 MP3 radio stations;
- all this has happened in less than one year!

What are your future marketing plans?

We have some interesting ideas, but we're trying to concentrate on getting more exposure outside the MP3.com site. For example, we're almost ready to announce a strategic agreement with a startup Web site which will offer a fantastic health spa facility on the Web. As the draft press release says:

> "This cooperation establishes Transoceanic as the primary source of musical material for Well-Living.com. To enhance its relaxing and rejuvenating qualities, Well-Living.com will use Transoceanic's life-enhancing music throughout the wellness spa, which includes animated instruction, guided meditation, and multi-sensory wellness experience centers."

We're very pleased about this tie-up because it provides us with a source of very well targeted listeners. In other words, the people that visit a site like Well-Living.com will, by definition, be people who are very likely to have an interest in our music.

How do you market your music during live performances?

So far we've been an entirely Web-based band. However, we would love to do some concerts one day! Our music isn't exactly typical live concert material, but given the right "chill out" occasion it could be perfect.

In closing, can you give us your overall philosophy on music, online marketing, and the future of the independent musician online?

I think a lot is changing in the music business, and the Internet is proving to be a serious kick in the pants for the music establishment. How it all shakes down is very difficult to predict. What is for sure is that music on the Web is here to stay, and as long as there are innovative and democratic Web sites like MP3.com about, there will be musicians making money from it.

There are also two undeniable trends working in favor of the Web musician. Firstly recording your own high quality music at home is getting easier and cheaper, and secondly the Internet will become bigger and bigger. Sounds fantastic to me! Get in on it now, and ride that wave!!

Ernesto Cortazar - Pianist

http://www.ernestocortazar.com/

With over 1,000,000 page views, 4,000,000 downloads, and over 10,000 DAMS sold, Ernesto Cortazar is arguably one of the most impressive online success stories to date. EC has made over $100,000 selling his music online, and has been featured in the Wall Street Journal, The New York Times, and Yahoo Internet Life. Couple this with the fact that he and his son are among the nicest and most gracious people on this planet, makes their success well-deserved. This is their story.

How many hours per day do you spend marketing your music online?

It is a minimum of 12 hours a day. My son Ernesto Jr does it. It includes uploading new files for the site, songs, newsletters and the most important and effective key to online success: e-mail response.

Responding to each and every e-mail an online artist receives, is the main point of promotion because the response creates a chain of friendship. I always keep a close relationship with my fans and I really know what they do, what they like and the names, hobbies and activities of their family and friends. It is having a true relationship of friendship, but online.

To tell you the truth, feelings and emotions can be communicated more directly when you express them online. People become more truthful and trustful. I find it a great experience to live and maintain.

What are some of the most effective methods you have used?

The most effective methods I have used are creation of an extended and affordable catalogue of music, enhanced with attractive cover art and creation of a site for the CDs exposure with the help of the fans. This has been a very effective method of promotion because it allows the fans to interact with us. When fans give and get feedback, they feel that they are participating in the project with us.

We have followed this process for our different language sites with fans all over the world. It took a simple exchange of my CD collection to get the site translated into each language.

Do you find your offline efforts help to support your online marketing, and vice versa?

Yes of course, every offline marketing activity supports online success. Interviews, concerts, mouth to mouth promotion and all of our other outside exposure boosts our online goals.

In fact, online marketing has helped me achieve many more things offline. We have been contacted via e-mail by important offline media such as the *New York Times* and various magazines. They gave us the offline exposure we needed to reach people who didn't even knew we existed.

Right now we are just starting on the road to offline success. We already see that offline marketing is a totally different world from online.

Yes, offline efforts definitely help us a lot. In particular, our newsletters are eagerly received. Fans are constantly interested in new achievements, especially when those achievements have crossed the online frontier.

Can you offer any advice, tips, or tricks to new musicians just starting out in marketing their music online?

One of the most important (if not the most) strategy for promotion I have is the mouth to mouth marketing. I have built a close relationship with each of my fans and reached a special bonding of trust with them. I simply ask each fan to help me promote my music by recommending it to their friends and loved ones. In this manner, a chain begins... New fans tell me they knew about me from their cousin/friend/etc...

Another nice strategy is to keep existing fans updated with newsletters to remind them of our music. That is really important because people forget, and you have to keep them interested on your new material. We also use the payola option that MP3 gives us. In that process, if you are a new unknown artist, you can help yourself reach the charts in a quicker, easier way. That lets everyone know you exist. At that point, start uploading new songs and releasing more records. The MP3 payola option is very, very important.

The extension of music catalogue is a very important factor too. Artists have to create new material to increase their site's importance while offering better service than most sites. Fans like to know their favorite artists are composing new material specially for them. This interaction builds a magic bond between the artist and his followers.

All these ideas have given me great results but the biggest and MOST important factor for my success has been the fan/artist relationship... that's the key... Friendship is the most valuable treasure.

I receive almost 100 e-mails daily from "frands" (friends/fans). I know exactly who they are, what they do and who their family members are. Responding to the e-mails is an immense job but it is tremendously rewarding.

I really am convinced that keeping a close relationship with the people who follow your music is the key to all. It's no secret that, MP3.com created the perfect music world in which friendship, love, respect and interaction are the essential factors to gain online audience which will eventually transfer to the offline world.

Is there any type of music you think does particularly well in comparison to other types when marketing it online? For instance, country, rock, folk, new age, etc.?

I think electronic and easy listening music get a lot more audience than any other, but things change every day in MP3.com and I would not be surprised if a country, rock or folk artist suddenly became the # 1 Artist... That's what makes online exposure in MP3.com so interesting and special. There are no boundaries, no limits, really. I am the first to be surprised at what I have achieved and it is a pleasure to share my experiences with everybody.

What accomplishments are you especially proud of with regard to your online success?

Online marketing has given me a lot to be proud of. One of the biggest accomplishments I have reached were the Interviews with the New York Times and *Wall Street Journal* newspapers. Each was a great experience and each article gained the attention of a large number of people in the offline world.

We have participated in several special edition CDs in cooperation with computer magazines. Those CDs have been distributed in countries like Japan and Spain. Then there was the stunning fact that Delta Airlines wanted to discuss exposing my music in Delta daily flights all around the world through their "Sky Disc" CD-ROM.

We have accomplished articles, quotes and photographs in print media such as *Billboard Magazine, Yahoo Magazine, Business Magazine Canada, America Economic, Dow Jones Magazine, Gig Magazine* and CNNenEspanol.com. We have even had the opportunity to sponsor three children through the World Vision Child Sponsorship Program.

All of these achievements have given me great pleasure and happiness, but the most life-enhancing accomplishment is the opportunity to meet special and interesting people all over the world. These people give me the most valuable dream-come-true... knowing my music is with them, beside them when they cry, when they smile... while they live...

This incredible personal feedback has resulted in

- 4,000,000 downloads of my music

- the satisfaction of selling more than 7,500 CDs in less than one year of operation.

In fact I am extremely happy because on August 19, 2000, I celebrated my first anniversary on MP3.com. Shortly after that anniversary, my two sites surpassed 1,000,000 page views! These are records no other independent artist has achieved online.

What are your future marketing plans?

At the moment I am finishing the first sheet music book for my songs and it will be distributed through MP3.com. It has been a huge project and I'm very happy that we are about to release it. Our fans have asked for it and they are anxiously expecting it.

Another upcoming marketing plan is signing a contract with a management company for concert booking around the world. This is one of the most important marketing steps we will deal this year. First I must thank my son, manager and promoter Ernesto Cortazar Jr. and the staff at Tazzar Studio for their tremendous promotion work. Second, I thank our fans all over the world for their outstanding support and feedback.

Our future marketing includes Christmas and special anniversary edition concerto albums. Then I will make my first music video and a tour of the U.S. West Coast.

How do you market your music during live performances?

When I do live performances, I simply recommend MP3.com's site to the audience telling them it is the place where they can get my CDs and that's all, I do not force anything, people like to enjoy and not receive any pressure during a show. That is very important to gain their trust and friendship. Removing the sales pressure carries the performance to a classier level because no sell is involved. Then the audience becomes interested in the product and asks for the place to buy it.

In closing, can you give us your overall philosophy on music, online marketing, and the future of the independent musician online?

My philosophy on music has always been to enjoy it as it is. I enjoy my music as it is created and I express it from the heart, even when I know the music will have no commercial future. I create the music that I feel at the moment. I feel that every art form should be respected, because artistic ideas arrive and should be developed without thought of commerce. After the development has been completed, the artist can turn his mind to the possible commercial aspects.

Online marketing is the future, and I see a time when everything is controlled and distributed through the Internet. The world is now contracted. All the things you once had to buy or get in the outside world, are now in the palm of your hand and just one click away. There you have the importance and the potential of online marketing. There are no boundaries and no limits. Right now you can be in an online meeting in Japan. Two hours later, you can be discussing a new project with executives of Australia. That's how things work online, that's the future.

I really think the future of independent musicians online will grow in a gigantic way. We are seeing it today. Record labels are merging due to expensive costs of promotion and distribution. Human staff is being cut from offices all around the world and sites like MP3.com are giving unsigned artists better exposure and greater benefits than they could ever expect from a record label. As I said before, we are living the future, and I bet that it won't be long until everyone worldwide will be buying not only CDs, but everything through a computer.

Kristin Banks

http://www.kristinbanks.com/

A Connecticut native now residing in San Diego, Kristin Banks is catching the attention of many industry pros. She is a consistent top seller on MP3.com and other Internet sites, commanding the #1 song spot three times in a row.

How many hours per day do you spend marketing your music online?

One or two at this point, but originally closer to 6.

What are some of the most effective methods you have used?

MP3.com has definitely been the most effective site for us.

Do you find your offline efforts help to support your online marketing, and vice versa?

To a small degree, yes. I suppose it mostly matters how many people you are able to reach offline who will follow up with a look at your Web site. In the other direction, our offline marketing hasn't helped as much because the Internet audience is a global one and it isn't easy for an indie to make the most of that kind of exposure.

Can you offer any advice, tips, or tricks to new musicians just starting out in marketing their music online?

Get on as many sites as you can as long as they have non-exclusive arrangements. Even if you are only getting a few looks/listens per day it's more than you'd have otherwise, and you can always direct people to a central location to share more information (i.e., www.yourband.com).

Is there any type of music you think does particularly well compared to other types when marketing it online? For instance, country, rock, folk, new age, etc.?

Electronic music seems to do quite well, probably because it's very popular with people in the age group of the average surfer and with people heavily into technology.

What accomplishments are you especially proud of with regard to your online success?

I've been selected for several compilation CDs on various Web sites, and have had three #1 songs on MP3.com, in addition to being featured on MP3.com several times. The exposure I've gained through the Internet has opened a lot of doors in the "real world" as well with publishing and management companies.

What are your future marketing plans?

We'll keep focusing on the Internet primarily, as it is a very cost-effective method of marketing to a large number of people.

How do you market your music during live performances?

We try to do the "soft sell" as much as possible. No need to guilt trip people into buying your music with calls to "support local music." As long as people know CDs are available at the store or on the Web site that's good enough for us.

In closing, can you give us your overall philosophy on music, online marketing, and the future of the independent musician online?

Indie musicians are frequently reminded that marketing and sales are very intellectual pursuits, quite unlike writing music. Music is all about emotion and feelings, and it can be hard to shift gears into "business mode." A talented manager is essential, even for bands trying to market their music primarily online. Certainly online marketing is already a staple for both indies and "label" bands, and is likely to become the primary way to sell music as well. A strong Internet presence is critical for ANY band.

Faith Rivera

http://faithgroove.com

Sample of artist Faith Rivera's Web site

As a solo artist, Faith Rivera has wowed audiences from Hawaii to California with Funky Gypsy (explosive female dance group) backing her soulful sounds with powerful choreography. Faith has shared the stage with Sheila E., Luther Vandross, Jon Secada, Deborah Cox, Morris Day & the Time, De La Soul, and Speech (Arrested Development.)

How many hours per day do you spend marketing your music online?

On the average, 1-2 hours per day. When I have more time or a particular project to push, it could be up to 4-5 hours.

What are some of the most effective methods you have used?

E-mailing my fan database with monthly newsletters; putting my URL on every letter; promo; e-mail that I send out; and in general, spreading word of my site daily whether it be online or offline.

Do you find your offline efforts help to support your online marketing, and vice versa?

Yes they definitely reinforce each other. In the case of my Latin project (mp3.com/lacarpool), our radio airplay both on and offline bring people to our site all the time. I'm sure that when we start performing live, the online fan database we've created will support our performances. We've already had people all around the world, Latin America to Europe, asking when we'll be swinging by.

Can you offer any advice, tips, or tricks to new musicians just starting out in marketing their music online?

Make it a point to tell one new person or company about your site every day. It might be handing out promos/biz cards with your URL to people you meet, or seeking out your specific market on the Web and asking for reviews, features, and airplay.

Definitely, creating or knowing your niche will help you get and keep an audience that is completely into what you're doing. Don't try to just enter the pop market - help yourself and the listener by choosing a very specific part of the pop market. For example, you might choose the new age/instrumental genre, or the growing genre of world beat, or you could tap into the girl power market.

Is there any type of music you think does particularly well compared to other types when marketing it online?

Certainly, the more specific your niche the more successful. Major labels & radio already provide the TOP 40. Success is found in providing something the listeners can't readily find elsewhere. For instance, I think this is the reason for LA Carpool's success - it has Latin grooves (specifically Salsa), with pop melodies sung in English which people can relate to, and my soulful vocals & electric rock guitar to add spice. Currently, people are just discovering or are seeking out this new Latin sound.

What accomplishments are you especially proud of with regard to your online success?

I'm proud to be a part of LA Carpool. The band has not performed live at all, but continually receives hits and praise from listeners all around the world. We receive positive reviews ranging from authentic Latin/salsa magazines and writers all the way to more pop/commercial critics.

As for my own solo material (http://mp3.com/faith), I'm proud each time one of my ballads personally uplifts a listener enough to write to me saying thanks. One Chinese listener, who probably didn't even understand the English text, said "Thank you for giving me someone to be close to." The Internet and the computer may seem cold & lifeless to the eye, but that combination has allowed me, or at least my music, to connect with people at the deepest levels.

What are your future marketing plans?

My future marketing plans include live performances, and of course even more material. LA Carpool will soon release our second album of salsa/rock hits and will promote both albums through live shows. It's important to constantly keep plugging away - promoting the site (the URL), getting reviews and features, radio play on and off the net. It's also vital to keep a database of all fans that e-mail us and also keep them informed of new developments.

How do you market your music during live performances?

First - you should definitely have a banner with your URL on it as well as the band name, or at the very least mention your name and your URL often during the performance. Also, you need a way for people to sign up for your mailing list.

Finally, you must make it easy for everyone to purchase your music at that moment or to purchase it online. Selling merchandise with your logo and URL is very helpful too.

In closing, can you give us your overall philosophy on music, online marketing, and the future of the independent musician online?

The Internet has given those of us who are independent musicians an effective, far-reaching tool to share our music & connect with listeners. In a very spiritual sense, I believe music does not belong to one person. Everyone should have access to it, and if it is advertisers to pay for this service...why not? All you can do is KNOW yourself and what you are trying to communicate. Find those listeners who will connect with it or give your music enough exposure for potential fans to find you. Nurture your relationship with your fan base and always be grateful for the opportunity to enrich their lives and to receive their gift of support.

It's not really about the music - it's about that indescribable energy and connection that awakens, uplifts, moves the spirit in each of us. Do what you can to promote - then relax and trust that your music will reach the ears that need to hear it.

Be true to you :)

Andreas Viklund, Lagoona

www.energymusic.com/lagoona

Lagoona is a melodic dance/trance music band from northern Sweden. The two members, Andreas Viklund and Björn Karlsson, have been releasing free music on the net since 1997, and Lagoona is today one of the worlds top Internet bands.

How many hours per day do you spend marketing your music online?

In average, I spend 1-2 hours every day on promoting and marketing Lagoona. This includes updates of our homepage, sending newsletters, checking charts and so on.

What are some of the most effective methods you have used?

Getting our songs on major MP3 Web sites like Hugemp3archive.com, Dmusic.com and Mp3place.net has helped us a lot. Being the spotlight band on pages with lots of visitors brings us a lot of attention. Surfers who visit several sites, and find my group on all of them, will get curious, eventually. It is always better to spread your songs to two sites, than to stick with only one.

Do you find your offline efforts help to support your online marketing, and vice versa?

Definitely! When we play at clubs and events, we tell the crowd to download the songs from our Web page. And on the Web page, we tell people to come check us out on the clubs. It's the same thing here. The more places where people hear about us, the more curious they will get.

Can you offer any advice, tips, or tricks to new musicians just starting out in marketing their music online?

Don't rush! Start slow, don't set your expectations too high. It's hard to get big on the Internet. I was lucky, but many of my friends have waited several years for their chance. And it WILL come, just be patient. Start with telling your friends about your music, and ask them to spread the word. Put up some posters in your neighborhood, saying "Hey, I exist! Listen to my music at ..."

Is there any type of music you think does particularly better than other types when marketing it online? For instance, country, rock, folk, new age, etc.?

The biggest music genre today (online) is the electronic styles such as trance, dance...

Why? Because those are the most common music styles. I can name 100 great electronic artists, but I don't know more than a few good rock bands.

I guess the reason for this is that it takes no studio to make trance music. It can be made with only software and computers. You can't make a country song if you don't have a decent recording equipment. But of course, it's harder to get heard if you make trance, because of the huge competition.

What accomplishments are you especially proud of in regard to your online success?

I guess getting two songs up on the #1 spot of the entire MP3.com is our biggest success. Out of 80,000 artists and 500,000 songs (October, 2000), my group Lagoona was the #1 band. That is huge.

What are your future marketing plans?

The border between online marketing and offline marketing gets smaller all the time. We will keep on working the way we've always been, by spreading our music to lots of sites. As for the offline marketing, we will release a vinyl single to DJs around the world. But then again, that vinyl will be marketed online too. We will try to get on compilations, finding a label that wants to bring us to the offline music listeners (CD buyers, radio). Also, we will keep our homepage updated.

How do you market your music during live performances?

By telling the crowd that "This song can be downloaded for free at www.mp3.com/lagoonamusic." It works!

In closing, can you give us your overall philosophy on music, online marketing, and the future of the independent musician online?

Music is not all about money. Music is a part of our lives. The most important aspect for me personally has not been making money. It's been to get heard! I want people to hear my songs, listen to them and let me know what they think. A mail in my inbox saying "I love your music" means more to me than any money. If more artists thought like this, we'd have less hyper-commercial bands and more real music out there. If everybody goes for the money, there will be no independent musicians out there. Online marketing will increase, not only when it comes to music but in everything else. I still hope, and think, that the "Free Music" spirit will stay alive.

Sergey Pimenov, PPK

pimenov@ppk.ru
http://english.ppk.ru
http://www.mp3.com/ppk

The Russian group PPK has taken the online world by storm. Its dance tracks have garnered an international reputation, and their downloads are consistently the highest rated on the large music sites. Ten years ago, it would not even be conceivable a group from behind the iron curtain could market their music to the world, but much has changed. Sergey Pimenov granted us this insightful interview from Russia.

How many hours per day do you spend marketing your music online?

I am online constantly, but for marketing our music I spend only 2 or 3 hours a day. In addition, I reply to letters in our site's forum and talk with our fans through ICQ.

What are some of the most effective methods you have used?

We try to use all known methods to promote our Web site (e.g., the registration in search systems, in FFA link lists.) Besides we have own maillist with a regular news posting. We try to reply to all letters from fans.

In our opinion the most effective method seems to be a link in a popular site or review in a popular magazine. The broadcast of our first video clip on Russia's MTV also helped us very much. We used computer graphics in the form of our URLs. That caused the permanent arrival of Internet visitors from Russia to our Web site. Suddenly daily Web traffic increased from 1000 to 7500.

Unfortunately we still aren't sure exactly how that happened. :))

We are sure that the main condition for Web site promotion is Music. If your music is good - people will find it.

Do you find your offline efforts help to support your online marketing, and vice versa?

Yes, our offline efforts create the base for our future fans and our site's visitors.

Can you offer any advice, tips, or tricks to new musicians just starting out in marketing their music online?

Advice is easy enough: use all possible methods to promote your Web site. Then certainly mix with admirers, reply to their letters and be an active participant of a music community.

Is there any type of music you think does particularly well over the others when marketing it online? For instance, country, rock, folk, new age, etc?

No doubt, it's electronic dance music. This music is the most suitable for online promotion.

What accomplishments are you especially proud of with regard to your online success?

We are proud that we became number 2 in TOP40 Charts on http://www.MP3.com, and we appreciate the large number of DJs who are playing our discs all over the world. We are particularly proud of our popularity. We are well known both here in Russia and in the rest of the world, thanks to the Internet exclusively.

What are your future marketing plans?

Right now we are modernizing our official site www.ppk.ru and improving its English version at english.ppk.ru. Also, we are negotiating with several companies about the use of our music in various places - on different sites, on vinyl discs and CD.

How do you market your music during live performances?

We don't sell our music on CD in Russia. There is too much piracy in Russia and selling CDs in Russia is not practical for artists here. The Internet became our distribution medium and takes the place of traditional distribution methods for us.

Is there any attempt at censorship at all from the Russian government?

No, never. It seems to me that our government does not pay much attention to life on the Internet. Music hasn't been subject to censorship in Russia for a long time. You can sing and do everything you want.

What is the Internet connection like in Russia?

It isn't very good :). The connection is really good only in Moscow - I use 56K and I am glad basically. But in other places it isn't so good. The phone lines in Russia are bad, but dial up is still the most widespread access type here.

How do you manage to sell your music/accept payment from America while located in Russia?

We have many friends in the US and they help us to manage this. To open an account in a bank within Russia and to receive money from abroad is a very complicated task. Russian banks don't understand how it could be possible - to get money "from whoever on the Internet" :)

Has Michel Gorbachov downloaded your music yet?

Sure! He does this daily!

In closing, can you give us your overall philosophy on music, online marketing, and the future of the independent musician online?

In our opinion the music is a product that people would like to get for free at all times. And Internet became the catalyst, accelerating the changes in a world model of music distribution. The Internet also changed everyone's ideas about the scope of distribution.

Only two years ago we couldn't dream for our music to be heard in thousand of places in the world. We couldn't picture our music making the money for us, allowing us to devote ourselves to the creation of new music. We couldn't picture the Internet giving us a chance to mix DIRECTLY with people who love our music.

No doubt, musicians will be more independent in future and there will be fewer barriers between the musicians and the fans of their music.

Micah Solomon

http://www.oasisCD.com

Micah Solomon is President of Oasis CD Duplication. Oasis is one of the first CD duplication companies to do its own radio promotion, and then to take the move toward providing your clients with a distribution channel. You must see a great future in indie marketing!

Give us an overview of your strategy:

Many of our clients are refugees from larger labels, and many others have never been on a label in the first place. We provide both types of artists with national radio promotion on our Oasis Sampler(tm) CD compilations. They are divided by genre--we have:

> Oasis Acoustic (which is subdivided into Celtic, Traditional, Humor, Kids, etc.),

> OasisAlternative, OasisRockandRoots, OasisUrban, OasisJazz,

> OasisWorld, OasisNewAge, and OasisCountry samplers.

They go to radio nationwide--up to 500 stations, depending on the genre. Artists are then provided with our proprietary, carefully-screened radio mailing list so they can follow up directly to see if the stations are interested in them specifically.

As far as distribution, our distribution program gets artists into the Valley Media catalog--which means their CD will be for sale at Amazon.com, CDnow, Barnes and Noble (bn.com), Buy.com, and almost every single other Internet superstore.

As you well know, this kind of mainstream distribution would have been literally impossible to obtain just a few years ago without being on a major or large indie label.

Tell us a little bit about your background as a musician:

I'm a keyboard player, songwriter, and singer. My music has been featured on National Public Radio (NPR) and other outlets. I also was a recording engineer for several years and was Executive Producer on one of Jerry Garcia's last efforts—a lovely instrumental CD he did with Sanjay Mishra entitled "Blue Incantation."

Oasis really seems to go the distance for the indie artist. Tell us some of the services your company offers musicians who want to press their own CD and sell it online:

See above for a description of our Oasis Sampler and national distribution programs. In addition we offer retail display boxes at no extra charge, and the all-important free barcode with every order.

Are cassettes still a good way to go, in addition to CDs?

For many musicians, cassettes are fine. Here's the scoop on cassettes. Don't make them if you play jazz or classical. These two genres are so dependent on dynamic range (the distance between the quiet parts and the loud parts) that cassettes have fallen completely out of favor because of their inherently high noise floor.

If you play any other genre of music, you should very likely make cassettes. Here's why: a lot of people want to hear you on the way back from your gig, and they may not have a CD player in their car. Some people only like you $10 worth, not $15 worth. It's important to offer things in different price ranges.

Believe it or not, many DJs program their shows in their cars and may not have a CD player. (Of course, you must also send a CD to DJs, as that's all you can get airplay for these days.)

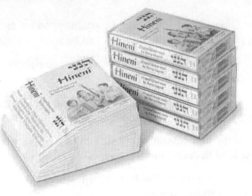

The Cassette is still a popular format

Note: If you make music for kids or do spoken-word material, you MUST make cassettes. Cassettes outsell CDs in these two genres by a wide margin.

How do you envision the future of the music business, and music distribution and marketing in general, as it relates to the indie artist?

I think it's clear that the music industry has become more democratized-- and will continue in that direction. However, there will become more and more of a need for "gatekeepers" to separate the weak from the strong musical offerings. So eventually there may be a backlash against what is well on its way to becoming a very democratized industry. But all in all, the trends are very, very positive for independent musicians--just make sure your graphics, your recording, your performance, and --absolutely crucial-- your songs are top-notch. Then bust your ass doing all the promotion you can think of.

How does Oasis differ from its competitors, purely from the manufacturing standpoint? (quality, price, etc.)

We are the only major replication company to offer single-speed (audiophile) glass cutting to clients who request it, and for a very modest fee. (Many mastering experts and "golden ears" types believe single speed mastering is the highest quality available, yet the music industry has refused to offer it because of the added time and expense it involves.)

- We offer a stunning and unprecedented assortment of packaging options:
    - the Oasis Jewel-Free Box (a patent-pending cardboard package supported by a plastic tray that can be used as a mailer)
    - the Oasis Rough-Look (brown paper bag-looking, very-recycled cardboard packaging),
    - the Oasis Soft-Spot (eight [!] panels of full color graphics with your CD suspended on an adorable little foam hub)
    - our wild new aluminum-coated mirror trays, which add a whole new look to conventional jewel box packaging.

- Our printing is done at 200 line screen, where the industry standard is 25% lower: 150 line screen.

- We are transitioning to direct-to-plate printing for better integrity.

- All of our CD replication is ISO-9002 certified.

- We have a long and very strong financial history, which means we won't go out of business before your project is complete. (Believe me, this happens every single day of the week in the music business, so it is an important consideration.)

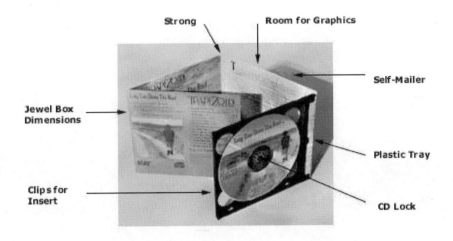

Strong

Room for Graphics

Self-Mailer

Jewel Box
Dimensions

Plastic Tray

Clips for
Insert

CD Lock

Oasis offers a unique alternative to jewelboxes

Micah Solomon <micah@oasisCD.com>
President, Oasis CD & Cassette Duplication
Micah's direct e-mail:micah@oasisCD.com
Toll-free:(888)BY-OASIS (888/296-2747)
Telephone from overseas: (540)675-1500
Fax:(540)675-2500
Address: 659 Zachary Taylor Hwy.(Box 721), Flint Hill, VA 22627 USA
Homepage (Winner, Luckman's Best of the Web) http://www.oasisCD.com
Proud Supporter of Folk Alliance, Indiegrrl, and AFIM

14
Setting Up Your Home-Based Digital Music Studio

Although the focus of this book is on marketing, you may find it valuable to read a short chapter on setting up the home digital studio. I know that many of you will be producing the work you are marketing on your own equipment, and the quality of the sound will have some effect on your sales.

With the proliferation of recording and computer gear coming out each week, it's become impossible to keep up with the changes as they happen, but standards do exist at any given time.

When I set up my own digital home studio, I had many questions, so I consulted with a local record producer and recording engineer. I also did quite a bit of research on what I could accomplish with a small budget. I figured that $6000 was all I could really afford, so I searched to find something I could do in that price range.

My goal was to get the best possible sound for the least dollars, yet do it in a format that would remain flexible down the road for taking into larger studios for expansion of track format or remixes.

Here is what I found.

Multitrack Recorders

All-in-one digital multitrackers are attractive in price and convenience, as they feature a built-in hard drive multitracker, EQ, effects, and a mixing board in one portable unit. They are easy to operate, and allow you to interface a CD burner for mastering.

Some vendors offer cost effective digital studio packages

But the glossy brochures don't mention they do not offer the best solution in terms of sound quality and flexibility. These console-type devices normally offer 8-16 tracks of digital multitracking, and record onto an internal hard drive, keeping the final tracks system-exclusive.

The difficulty with these units right now is that in order to fit as many tracks as possible on a small hard drive, they use compression schemes to record their tracks. They record their tracks at a lower bit-sampling rate than can be achieved through a stand-alone ADAT using S-VHS tape.

The trade off in money and convenience is in the final sonic result, for you have no control over the compression and bit sampling rate as your tracks are being saved.

Does this make an audible difference? Yes. If you are pitching your material to industry pros, their trained ears do hear the difference.

But if you are concerned with primarily selling your music directly online, this quality difference is not likely to be noticed by the average listener or consumer. I say this with caution, though, because the line is blurring quickly.

Keep in mind that as digital recording systems become more and more affordable, capable of higher quality sound for a lower price, they then become more accessible to the home musician. Thus, the bar on acceptable sonic quality is raised. An indie CD that was recorded a year ago when the sonic quality was considered state of the art at that time, might now be considered "old hat."

The other difficulty with these systems is their closed architecture. If you took a submix of these tracks to a larger studio, you would have to bring the entire unit with you to do a dump onto their existing systems. You would not be able to sync your tracks to the master tape, and you would be limited in sonic quality.

Stand-alone units have their advantages, but in our view, from a cost vs. quality standpoint, you are better off with separate components.

Mixing Boards

Some boards, such as PA boards, can be noisy, meaning they introduce a lot of line or signal noise into the audio. That's why a quiet board designed for recording is your best option. I have found that Mackie and Behringer offer the best results for the money.

Behringer 24 channel 4 bus console - An outstanding buy

Microphones

A good mike is essential, but you don't have to buy an expensive one to get great sound. When I shopped for my mike, I took a recording engineer down to the local Guitar Center, and paid him $75 to test mikes with me for about an hour.

We proceeded to test microphones using the A/B method, plugging each microphone into the same cable and channel, eq'd flat, and listening over headphones.

After testing over 50 mikes in all price ranges, we both came to the conclusion that many of the higher priced mikes did not sound as good as some of the lower priced mikes. Of course, the Neumann microphones produced superior results, but the price tag did not justify the sound quality, for I found a much lower priced mike with almost equal frequency response for many times less.

I chose an AKG C2000B as my centerpiece microphone for both vocals and recording acoustic instruments, and to both my ears and the recording engineer's, it sounds almost as good as a Neumann tube mike!

My ideal recording solution was:

- 2 Alesis 8 track ADAT recorders
- Behringer 24x4 channel mixing board
- Alesis Nanoverb and MicroCompressor
- Hewlett Packard CD-Writer with Alesis CD-Sync Software
- AKG C2000B Microphone

I put together my studio for just under $6000, with all the cables and software included, and the sonic result is astounding.

The ADAT format on S-VHS format tape allows complete synchronization with most studio environments, and allows more flexibility in terms of mixdown and backwards and forwards compatibility. The sound is flawless and noise-free, and allows for a great deal of latitude with exchanging tapes with other studios and musicians.

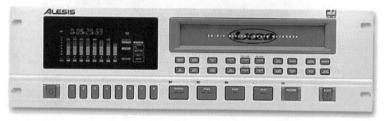

ADAT-LX20 20 Bit Digital Audio Recorder

Recording Room

I do not believe that you need an acoustically sound-proof room with baffles and sound dividers and a high ceiling. I learned recording from an engineer who recorded all of his masters in his bedroom studio, and it was often noisy during takes.

He had a technique of miking and recording that was innovative and unique. He was able to pinpoint noise sources and eliminate them, or mike in a way that would block out the noise. Now of course, you can't have screaming kids in the room with you, or airplanes landing on the roof, but the point here is that you don't need a completely quiet environment to get good recordings.

I have set up recording studios in apartments, bathrooms, and even a walk-in closet, and achieved superb results. Using innovation and imagination, you can do it too.

Hard Drive Computer Recording

Very good results can be achieved using a computer and a software package such as ProTools, but again, keep in mind that lack of flexibility can sometimes be a problem. Not only is the computer solution expensive, what if you decide you want to go into a larger studio and dump your tracks to analog, or a larger drive system? Then it's time to pack all your CPU's, and make that long, difficult journey with all your drives in tow.

When you add up the cost of hard drive recording and the memory and software required to do it, you would be better off using the ADAT solution, and keeping multiple backup copies of your work. It's much simpler to make a copy of a S-VHS than it is to back up 20 gigs of hard drive data.

15
Making It All Happen: a Final Word

Do you have what it takes to market your music on the Internet, each and every day? If you do, and you apply the principles outlined in this book, you are well on your way to finding your fortune on the World Wide Web.

It all starts with you. You must be a self-starting, motivated individual with the drive and determination, and the willingness to succeed.

Your own future now rests squarely in your hands. Will you move from a potential to a reality? Will your own hand be the guide that takes you from where you are now to the pinnacle of whatever you define as your success?

And what about your inner objective?

No book on marketing, in my view, could be complete without a personal philosophy or vision. Many of us are motivated by different criteria, but our psychology of basic human needs remains the same.

Whatever your goals are in this business of music, always keep in mind that bringing joy to others through the power of your music is the ultimate end.

Doing it your way means that the channels through which you would have traditionally needed to pass are open, the filters are off, and your music can be marketed directly to the consumer.

This brings to bear the question of influence. Your music, and hence, your message is passed directly on to the listening public, and this can become a double-edged sword.

Will you use it responsibly?

By listening to some of the messages of much of our urban rap today, I'm dismayed that many young people haven't. In my view, our society has enough violence, hate, and terror in it. Keep your messages positive, encouraging, and without malice.

It is my personal philosophy that "making it" is more about the journey than the destination. Sometimes we become so caught up in our zeal to make money that we forget that the entire process is about the doing, and not the getting.

In our western view, the acquisition of wealth and power seems to be the measure of success. This contrasts with my view that the measure of success is the quality of the methods used to arrive at success.

I believe that there should always be a personal vision or philosophy at work in all motivational behavior, no matter what the goal. By defining the message that you want to deliver, and defining the ethics and spiritual principles you use to achieve that end, you will always be in control of the ultimate measure of your success.

No outer success can equal the inner success needed to be truly happy.

I wish all of you the very greatest of success and hope that this book will help you to achieve your most profound dreams.

Appendix 1
Merchant Account Providers and Third Party Credit Card Processors

The list below has been collected to help you find financial institutions to process credit cards. Where possible, instead of referring to any individual sales rep, we have listed the company headquarters or a central referral number.

Be sure to compare the rates and terms offered by each company in this list and from other sources before making a decision about what financial organization to use to process charge cards.

Merchant Account Sources

Banks

Some banks will accept home businesses and mail order businesses for merchant accounts. Ask first at your own bank, then ask at other commercial banks in your area. Focus on some of the smaller ones that seem to target small businesses.

If they will accept you, compare their rates to those of some of the third party providers listed below.

Professional Associations

Some associations have affiliations with banks or with third party providers who accept their members for merchant status. Again, compare the rates you get this way to those you can get on your own. The cost of equipment, discount fees or application fees may be higher through the association than from other sources.

Organizations that work with small and home businesses:

Alta Financial Services
1839 Alma School Road, Suite 226
Mesa, AZ 852-10
1-800-684-4010 or 602-491-4010
Fax: 602-491-4910
Accepts home and small business.

Chittenden Bank
merchantsvc@chittenden.com
Accepts small and home businesses and Internet
businesses. Internet businesses must use secured
transactions such as CyberCash and products must not be delivered online.

Card Service International
Headquarters:
26775 Malibu Hills Road
Agura hills CA 91301
1-800- 456- 5989
Accepts home and small business. Accepts some with marginal credit. Rates
and fees seemed to vary and to depend partly on what sales rep was contacted.

EMS Global (ECHO network)
Electronic Merchant Systems- Global
E.9212 Montgomery, Suite 202
Spokane, WA 99206
1-800-757-5453 or 1-509-924-6812
Accepts home business, small business, mail order. Considers those with poor
credit ratings. Requires you to have a checking account with them. Money from
transactions is deposited in that account. You have to withdraw the money (cash
a check) when you want to take the money out..

Executive Bankcard Services
4113 Scotts Valley Dr. suite 100
Scotts Valley, CA 95066
831 440-1437 Fax 831 440-1433
Contact-Matthew Swinnerton
Accepts a wide variety of home-based and small businesses.

Merchant Bankcard Network
151 Route 33 East Manalapan, NJ 07726
1-800-708-4494
Accepts home-based, mail order, Internet business. Considers businesses with
credit problems.

NaBanco/First Data Merchant
Headquarters
PO Box 6600 Hagesrtown MD, 21741
Phone: 1-800-359-3559
Retail and professional home businesses. Mail order and home business would
require 2 years in business and good financials according to a sales rep for the
company. No Internet transactions. New retailers not a problem.

Novus Network Services (Formerly Discover Card)
1-800-347-7763

Teleflora CreditLine
12233 West Olympic Blvd.
Los Angeles, CA 90064
New Accounts/Sales
1 800-480-6694
Accepts home-based and mail order businesses.

Discounted credit card processing equipment and software:

Web site: http://www.MerchantWarehouse.com

Third Party Processors

These companies charge you to collect funds on your behalf, and often provide additional benefits, such as database management and affiliate sales program administration/bookkeeping.

CCBill
http://www.ccbill.com

WebCharge
http://www.Web-charge.com/

Site Check
http://sitecheck.com/exclu.htm

Sitekey
http://www.sitekey.com/

Verotel
http://www.verotel.com/index.html

Automated Transactions Corp.
http://www.atcbilling.com/

Pay By Web
http://www.paybyWeb.com/

CreditPro
http://www.CreditPro.Com/

Appendix 2
Music Publications and
Online Music Sites

Billboard Online
http://www.billboard.com/

Wall of Sound — comprehensive site featuring artist pages, interviews, news and reviews, charts, new releases.
http://wallofsound.go.com/

Rolling Stone Magazine — Venerable consumer music mag.
http://www.rollingstone.com/

Launch.com — daily music news, concert reviews, music videos, audio clips.
http://www.launch.com/

New Musical Express — Blend of music reviews, news, and live gig listings.
http://www.nme.com/

RootsWorld — world music; roots, folk, the music made by people for people.
http://www.rootsworld.com/rw/rw.html

Fused — Best of the underground music scene in the UK. Record, club, video, film
& event reviews and interviews.
http://www.fused.com/

Dotmusic — online magazine with the latest band profiles, music industry news, official UK charts, US radio charts, and the chance to buy CDs.
http://www.dotmusic.com/

Addicted to Noise — interviews with major artists, album reviews and music news.
http://www.addict.com/

Appendix 3
Usenet:
An Approximate Description

by Chip Salzenberg

Usenet is a world-wide distributed discussion system. It consists of a set of "newsgroups" with names that are classified hierarchically by subject. Articles" or "messages" are "posted" to these newsgroups by people on computers with the appropriate software -- these articles are then broadcast to other interconnected computer systems via a wide variety of networks. Some newsgroups are "moderated"; in these newsgroups, the articles are first sent to a moderator for approval before appearing in the newsgroup. Usenet is available on a wide variety of computer systems and networks, but the bulk of modern Usenet traffic is transported over either the Internet or UUCP.

Why Is Usenet So Hard to Define?

The first thing to understand about Usenet is that it is widely misunderstood. Every day on Usenet, the "blind men and the elephant" phenomenon is evident, in spades. In my opinion, more flame wars arise because of a lack of understanding of the nature of Usenet than from any other source. And consider that such flame wars arise, of necessity, among people who are on Usenet. Imagine, then, how poorly understood Usenet must be by those outside!

Any essay on the nature of Usenet cannot ignore the erroneous impressions held by many Usenet users. Therefore, this article will treat falsehoods first. Keep reading for truth.(Beauty, alas, is outside the scope of this article.)

What Usenet Is Not

1. Usenet is not an organization.

No person or group has authority over Usenet as a whole. No one controls who gets a news feed, which articles are propagated where, who can post articles, or anything else. There is no "Usenet Incorporated," nor is there a "Usenet User's Group." You're on your own.

Granted, there are various activities organized by means of Usenet newsgroups. The newsgroup creation process is one such activity. But it would be a mistake to equate Usenet with the organized activities it makes possible. If they were to stop tomorrow, Usenet would go on without them.

2. Usenet is not a democracy.

Since there is no person or group in charge of Usenet as a whole -- i.e. there is no Usenet "government" -- it follows that Usenet cannot be a democracy, autocracy, or any other kind of "-acy." (But see "The Camel's Nose?" below.)

3. Usenet is not fair.

After all, who shall decide what's fair? For that matter, if someone is behaving unfairly, who's going to stop him? Neither you nor I, that's certain.

4. Usenet is not a right.

Some people misunderstand their local right of "freedom of speech" to mean that they have a legal right to use others' computers to say what they wish in whatever way they wish, and the owners of said computers have no right to stop them.

Those people are wrong. Freedom of speech also means freedom not to speak. If I choose not to use my computer to aid your speech, that is my right. Freedom of the press belongs to those who own one.

5. Usenet is not a public utility.

Some Usenet sites are publicly funded or subsidized. Most of them, by plain count, are not. There is no government monopoly on Usenet, and little or no government control.

6. Usenet is not an academic network.

It is no surprise that many Usenet sites are universities, research labs or other academic institutions. Usenet originated with a link between two universities, and the exchange of ideas and information is what such institutions are all about. But the passage of years has changed Usenet's character. Today, by plain count, most Usenet sites are commercial entities.

7. Usenet is not an advertising medium.

Because of Usenet's roots in academia, and because Usenet depends so heavily on cooperation (sometimes among competitors), custom dictates that advertising be kept to a minimum. It is tolerated if it is infrequent, informative, and low-hype.

The "comp.newprod" newsgroup is NOT an exception to this rule: product announcements are screened by a moderator in an attempt to keep the hype-to-information ratio in check.

If you must engage in flackery for your company, use the "biz" hierarchy, which is explicitly "advertising-allowed", and which (like all of Usenet) is carried only by those sites that want it.

8. Usenet is not the Internet.

The Internet is a wide-ranging network, parts of which are subsidized by various governments. It carries many kinds of traffic, of which Usenet is only one. And the Internet is only one of the various networks carrying Usenet traffic.

9. Usenet is not a UUCP network.

UUCP is a protocol (actually a "protocol suite," but that's a technical quibble) for sending data over point-to-point connections, typically using dialup modems. Sites use UUCP to carry many kinds of traffic, of which Usenet is only one. And UUCP is only one of the various transports carrying Usenet traffic.

10. Usenet is not a United States network.

It is true that Usenet originated in the United States, and the fastest growth in Usenet sites has been there. Nowadays, however, Usenet extends worldwide.

The heaviest concentrations of Usenet sites outside the U.S. seem to be in Canada, Europe, Australia and Japan.

Keep Usenet's worldwide nature in mind when you post articles. Even those who can read your language may have a culture wildly different from yours. When your words are read, they might not mean what you think they mean.

11. Usenet is not a UNIX network.

Don't assume that everyone is using "rn" on a UNIX machine. Among the systems used to read and post to Usenet are Vaxen running VMS, IBM mainframes, Amigas, Macintoshes and MS-DOS PCs.

12. Usenet is not an ASCII network. The A in ASCII stands for "American". Sites in other countries often use character sets better suited to their language(s) of choice; such are typically, though not always, supersets of ASCII.

Even in the United States, ASCII is not universally used: IBM mainframes use (shudder) EBCDIC. Ignore non-ASCII sites if you like, but they exist.

13. Usenet is not software.

There are dozens of software packages used at various sites to transport and read Usenet articles. So no one program or package can be called "the Usenet software." Software designed to support Usenet traffic can be (and is) used for other kinds of communication, usually without risk of mixing the two. Such private communication networks are typically kept distinct from Usenet by the invention of newsgroup names different from the universally-recognized ones.

Well, enough negativity.

What Usenet Is

Usenet is the set of people who exchange articles tagged with one or more universally-recognized labels, called "newsgroups" (or "groups" for short). There is often confusion about the precise set of newsgroups that constitute Usenet; one commonly accepted definition is that it consists of newsgroups listed in the periodic "List of Active Newsgroups" postings which appear regularly in news.lists.misc and other newsgroups. A broader definition of Usenet would include the newsgroups listed in the article "Alternative Newsgroup Hierarchies" (frequently posted to news.lists.misc). An even broader definition includes even newsgroups that are restricted to specific geographic regions or organizations. Each Usenet site makes its own decisions about the set of groups available to its users; this set differs from site to site.

(Note that the correct term is "newsgroups"; they are not called areas, bases, boards, bboards, conferences, round tables, SIGs, echoes, rooms or usergroups! Nor, as noted above, are they part of the Internet, though they may reach your site over it. Furthermore, the people who run the news systems are called news administrators, not sysops. If you want to be understood, be accurate.)

Diversity

If the above definition of Usenet sounds vague, that's because it is. It is almost impossible to generalize over all Usenet sites in any non-trivial way. Usenet encompasses government agencies, large universities, high schools, businesses of all sizes, home computers of all descriptions, etc, etc. (In response to the above paragraphs, it has been written that there is nothing vague about a network that carries megabytes of traffic per day.I agree. But at the fringes of Usenet, traffic is not so heavy. In the shadowy world of news-mail gateways and mailing lists, the line between Usenet and not-Usenet becomes very hard to draw.)

Control

Every administrator controls his own site. No one has any real control over any site but his own. The administrator gets her power from the owner of the system she administers. As long as her job performance pleases the owner, she can do whatever she pleases, up to and including cutting off Usenet entirely. Them's the breaks.

Sites are not entirely without influence on their neighbors, however. There is a vague notion of "upstream" and "downstream" related to the direction of high-volume news flow. To the extent that "upstream" sites decide what traffic they will carry for their "downstream" neighbors, those "upstream" sites have some influence on their neighbors' participation in Usenet. But such influence is usually easy to circumvent; and heavy-handed manipulation typically results in a backlash of resentment.

Periodic Postings

To help hold Usenet together, various articles (including this one) are periodically posted in newsgroups in the "news" hierarchy. These articles are provided as a public service by various volunteers. They are few but valuable. Learn them well.

Among the periodic postings are lists of active newsgroups, both "standard" (for lack of a better term) and "alternative. "These lists are maintained by David Lawrence and periodically posted to the news.lists.misc newsgroup. They reflect his personal view of Usenet, and as such are not "official" in any sense of the word. However, if you're looking for a description of subjects discussed on Usenet, or if you're starting up a new Usenet site, David's lists are an eminently reasonable place to start.

Propagation

In the old days, when UUCP over long-distance dialup lines was the dominant means of article transmission, a few well-connected sites had real influence in determining which newsgroups would be carried where. Those sites called themselves "the backbone." But things have changed. Nowadays, even the smallest Internet site has connectivity the likes of which the backbone admin of yesteryear could only dream. In addition, in the U.S., the advent of cheaper long-distance calls and high-speed modems has made long-distance Usenet feeds thinkable for smaller companies.

There is only one pre-eminent site for UUCP transport of Usenet in the U.S., namely UUNET. But UUNET isn't a player in the propagation wars, because it never refuses any traffic. UUNET charges by the minute, after all; and besides, to refuse based on content might jeopardize its legal status as an enhanced service provider.

All of the above applies to the U.S. In Europe, different cost structures favored the creation of strictly controlled hierarchical organizations with central registries. This is all very unlike the traditional mode of U.S. sites (pick a name, get the software, get a feed, you're on).Europe's "benign monopolies," long uncontested, now face competition from looser organizations patterned after the U.S. model.

Newsgroup Creation

The document that describes the current procedure for creating a new newsgroup is entitled "How To Create A New Newsgroup. "Its common name, however, is "the guidelines." If you follow the guidelines, it is probable that your group will be created and will be widely propagated.

HOWEVER: Because of the nature of Usenet, there is no way for any user to enforce the results of a newsgroup vote (or any other decision, for that matter).Therefore, for your new newsgroup to be propagated widely, you must not only follow the letter of the guidelines; you must also follow its spirit. And you must not allow even a whiff of shady dealings or dirty tricks to mar the vote. In other words, don't tick off system administrators; they will get their revenge.

So, you may ask: How is a new user supposed to know anything about the "spirit" of the guidelines? Obviously, he can't. This fact leads inexorably to the following recommendation:

>> **If you are a new user, don't try to create a new newsgroup.** <<

If you have a good newsgroup idea, then read the "news.groups" newsgroup for a while (six months, at least) to find out how things work. If you're too impatient to wait six months, then you really need to learn; read "news.groups" for a year instead. If you just can't wait, find a Usenet old hand to help you with the request for discussion.(All votes are run by neutral third-party Usenet Volunteer Votetakers).

Readers may think this advice unnecessarily strict. Ignore it at your peril. It is embarrassing to speak before learning. It is foolish to jump into a society you don't understand with your mouth open. And it is futile to try to force your will on people who can tune you out with the press of a key.

The Camel's Nose?

As was observed above in "What Usenet Is Not," Usenet as a whole is not a democracy. However, there is exactly one feature of Usenet that has a form of democracy: newsgroup creation. A new newsgroup is unlikely to be widely propagated unless its sponsor follows the newsgroup creation guidelines; and the current guidelines require a new newsgroup to pass an open vote.

There are those who consider the newsgroup creation process to be a remarkably powerful form of democracy, since without any coercion, its decisions are almost always carried out. In their view, the democratic aspect of newsgroup creation is the precursor to an organized and democratic Usenet Of The Future.

On the other hand, some consider the democratic aspect of the newsgroup creation process a sham and a fraud, since there is no power of enforcement behind its decisions, and since there appears little likelihood that any such power of enforcement will ever be given it. For them, the appearance of democracy is only a tool used to keep proponents of flawed newsgroup proposals from complaining about their losses.

So, is Usenet on its way to full democracy? Or will property rights and mistrust of central authority win the day? Beats me.

If You Are Unhappy...

Property rights being what they are, there is no higher authority on Usenet than the people who own the machines on which Usenet traffic is carried. If the owner of the machine you use says, "We will not carry alt.sex on this machine," and you are not happy with that order, you have no Usenet recourse. What can we outsiders do, after all?

That doesn't mean you are without options. Depending on the nature of your site, you may have some internal political recourse. Or you might find external pressure helpful. Or, with a minimal investment, you can get a feed of your own from somewhere else. Computers capable of taking Usenet feeds are down in the $500 range now, UNIX-capable boxes are going for under $1000 (that price is dropping fast, so by the time you read this, it may already be out of date!) and there are several freely-redistributable UNIX-like operating systems (NetBSD, FreeBSD, 386BSD and Linux from ftp sites all around the world, complete with source code and all the software needed to run a Usenet site) and at least two commercial UNIX or UNIX-like systems in the $100 price range.

No matter what, though, appealing to "Usenet" won't help. Even if those who read such an appeal are sympathetic to your cause, they will almost certainly have even less influence at your site than you do. By the same token, if you don't like what some user at another site is doing, only the administrator and owner of that site have any authority to do anything about it. Persuade them that the user in question is a problem for them, and they might do something -- if they feel like it, that is.

If the user in question is the administrator or owner of the site from which she posts, forget it; you can't win. If you can, arrange for your news-reading software to ignore articles from her; and chalk one up to experience.

Appendix 4
Marketing
on the Usenet Hierarchy

by Mark Joyner - Aesop Corporation

What are They?

Newsgroups are world wide bulletin board systems organized by the Usenet news system. There are over 40,000 newsgroups available right now. You may not be able to access each one. It really depends on your Internet Provider. When a new newsgroup is formed, your IP may or may not choose to offer it.

If you need to access a group that is not offered by your provider, you can configure your newsreader to access a public access news server. Here are a couple of public access news servers and also a URL where you can find a more comprehensive list of the public servers:

> news.sexzilla.com

> news.caribsurf.com

> demonews.mindspring.com (read only, no posting)

If none of these work, follow the link below and try some of the over 800 listed there.

Extensive List of Public News Servers

You can also try these Web browser based news services.

> FeedME at http://www.feedme.com

> DejaNews at http://www.deja.com

Deja.Com offers easy access to newsgroup threads
(Deja.com has just been acquired by Google.com.)

As a Marketing Tool

There are two different ways to use the newsgroups and both are powerful. You can post simple advertisements or make contacts indirectly. There are some important things to consider in both methods so read carefully.

Simple Advertisements

This is the most common method for marketing on the newsgroups. Basically, this entails writing an ad and posting it on a newsgroup. Free advertisement for all, right? Well, it's not that simple. Firstly, most newsgroups don't care too much for unsolicited ads. In fact, you may get flamed or e-mail bombed or worse if you do this in some newsgroups. Generally, netiquette dictates that you only post messages related to that particular newsgroup. Don't despair, though. There are some newsgroups that welcome ads. Most of the business or MLM related newsgroups should be OK.

If in doubt, read several posts of a newsgroup to get the feel of it. Just because you see a bunch of ads doesn't mean it's OK, though. Some people will post ads anyway. I advise against this as it will probably do more harm than good.

Here is a list of some newsgroups where ads are generally OK. Remember not to use too much hype. Write a concise, informative ad; it will be far better received than a bunch of unprofessional hype.

1. <biz.*> This hierarchy of newsgroups generally welcomes ads. Each group is different, though so look before you post. Here are a few examples:

   biz.misc

   biz.general (see this group for posting suggestions and restrictions)

   Most groups that have words like "mlm", "business", "money" etc. in the title will be OK. Once again, be careful.

2. <alt.make.money> will gladly accept your post, but <rec.collecting.paper-money> probably won't be too interested in what your selling (unless it's paper money).

3. <comp.newprod> This group is moderated meaning that your message will have to be approved by the moderator. If what you're posting isn't about a new computer product, don't bother.

4. Most newsgroups that have .forsale or .marketplace somewhere in the title. Most of these are good for selling single items. Do a search and look around. For example:

   alt.forsale

   alt.marketplace.funky-stuff.forsale

5. <misc.forsale.*> This hierarchy is mainly used to place classified style ads like above. Commercial postings are probably not welcome.

Making Contacts

Another way to increase your presence in the newsgroups is less direct. It entails looking through the newsgroups and responding to existing discussion threads. I'm not proposing that you break into a thread and throw in your ad. This is highly unadvisable.

I am proposing something far less obtrusive and far more effective. There are several techniques you can use to make contacts, but essentially they can be divided into two categories: signature ads and prospect seeking.

1. Signature Ads

   This is a simple and effective technique. Here you respond to off topic threads with pertinent information. At the bottom of your post, include a little blurb about your business. Be sure to include URL, e-mail, and short description.

   Don't make this signature too long, this is considered bad netiquette. Also, don't just break into a thread to say something like "yeah, me too". If you don't have any genuine pertinent input, go find a thread that you can contribute to. Just getting involved in various threads will help build your name and build contacts online. You never know when one of these people will need your services. And as more people see your name, the larger brand presence you have.

2. Prospect Seeking

This is an extremely powerful technique. Basically, it entails searching the newsgroups for people who would be interested in your product. For instance, you sell silver widgets. You do a search on DejaNews for "silver widgets" and you find a post from someone who is "dying to find a silver widget, but can't find one." You run to the rescue! "I sell silver widgets and some mighty fine ones." You simply give them a URL, a number, and an e-mail address. Chances are, you probably just made a sale.

Little light bulbs are probably popping up around your head right now. There are many ways you can apply this powerful technique.

Appendix 5
Search Engine Placement Tips

by Danny Sullivan of SearchEngineWatch.com

A search engine query often turns up hundreds or thousands of matching Web pages. In most cases, only the 10 most "relevant" matches are displayed first. Naturally, anyone who runs a Web site wants to be in the "top ten" results. This is because most users will find a result they like in the top ten. Being listed 11 or beyond means that many people may miss your Web site.

The tips below will help you come closer to this goal, both for the keywords you think are important and for phrases you may not even be anticipating.

Pick Your Strategic Keywords

How do you think people will search for your Web page? The words you imagine them typing into the search box are your strategic keywords. For example, say you have a page devoted to stamp collecting. Anytime someone types "stamp collecting," you want your page to be in the top ten results. Then those are your strategic keywords for that page.

Each page in your Web site will have different strategic keywords that reflect the page's content. For example, say you have another page about the history of stamps. Then "stamp history" might be your keywords for that page.

Your strategic keywords should always be at least two or more words long. Usually, too many sites will be relevant for a single word, such as "stamps." This "competition" means your odds of success are lower. Don't waste your time fighting the odds. Pick phrases of two or more words, and you'll have a better shot at success.

The Researching Keywords article available to site subscribers provides additional information about selecting key terms.

Position Your Keywords

Make sure your strategic keywords appear in the crucial locations on your Web pages. The page title is most important. Failure to put strategic keywords in the page title is the main reason why perfectly relevant Web pages may be poorly ranked.

Search engines also like pages where keywords appear "high" on the page, as described more fully on the Search Engine Ranking page. To accommodate them, use your strategic keywords for your page headline, if possible. Have them also appear in the first paragraphs of your Web page.

Keep in mind that tables can "push" your text further down the page, making keywords less relevant because they appear lower on the page. This is because tables break apart when search engines read them. For example, picture a typical two-column page, where the first column has navigational links, while the second column has the keyword loaded text. Humans see that page like this:

Home Stamp Collecting

Page 1

Page 2 Stamp collection is worldwide experience.

Page 3 Thousands enjoy it everyday, and millions

Page 4 can be made from this hobby/business.

Search engines (and those with old browsers) see the page like this:

Home

Page 1

Page 2

Page 3

Page 4

Stamp Collecting

Stamp collection is worldwide experience. Thousands enjoy it everyday, and millions can be made from this hobby/business.

See how the keywords have moved down the page? There's no easy way around this, except to use meta tags. That helps for the search engines that use them. For the others, it may not be that big a problem. Consider how tables might affect your page, but don't necessarily stop using them. I like tables, and I'll continue to use them.

Large sections of JavaScript can also have the same affect as tables. The search engine reads this information first, which causes the normal HTML text to appear lower on the page. Place your script further down on the page, if possible. As with tables, the use of meta tags can also help.

Have Relevant Content

Changing your page titles and adding meta tags is not necessarily going to help your page do well for your strategic keywords if the page has nothing to do with the topic. Your keywords need to be reflected in the page's content.

In particular, that means you need HTML text on your page. Sometimes sites present large sections of copy via graphics. It looks pretty, but search engines can't read those graphics. That means they miss out on text that might make your site more relevant. Some of the search engines will index ALT text and comment information, along with meta tags. But to be safe, use HTML text whenever possible. Some of your human visitors will appreciate it, also.

Be sure that your HTML text is "visible." Some designers try to spam search engines by repeating keywords in a tiny font or in the same color at the background color to make the text invisible to browsers. Search engines are catching on to these and other tricks. Expect that if the text is not visible in a browser, then it won't be indexed by a search engine.

Finally, consider "expanding" your text references, where appropriate. For example, a stamp collecting page might have references to "collectors" and "collecting." Expanding these references to "stamp collectors" and "stamp collecting" reinforces your strategic keywords in a legitimate and natural manner. Your page really is about stamp collecting, but edits may have reduced its relevancy unintentionally.

Avoid Search Engine Stumbling Blocks

Some search engines see the Web the way someone using a very old browser might. They may not read image maps. They may not read frames. You need to anticipate these problems, or a search engine may not index any or all your Web pages.

Have HTML links

Often, designers create only image map links from the home page to inside pages. A search engine that can't follow these links won't be able to get "inside" the site. Unfortunately, the most descriptive, relevant pages are often inside pages rather than the home page.

Solve this problem by adding some HTML hyperlinks to the home page that lead to major inside pages or sections of your Web site. This is something that will help some of your human visitors, also. Put them down at the bottom of the page. The search engine will find them and follow them.

Also consider making a site map page with text links to everything in your Web site. You can submit this page, which will help the search engines locate pages within your Web site.

Finally, be sure you do a good job of linking internally between your pages. If you naturally point to different pages from within your site, you increase the odds that search engines will follow links and find more of your Web site.

Frames can kill

Some of the major search engines cannot follow frame links. Make sure there is an alternative method for them to enter and index your site, either through meta tags or smart design. For more information, see the tips on using frames.

Dynamic Doorblocks

Generating pages via CGI or database-delivery? Expect that some of the search engines won't be able to index them. Consider creating static pages whenever possible, perhaps using the database to update the pages, not to generate them on the fly. Also, avoid symbols in your URLs, especially the ? symbol. Search engines tend to choke on it.

Use Meta Tags

As mentioned above, meta tags can help you overcome problems with tables, frames and other trouble areas. Meta tags will also help you control your site's description in engines that support them. You should use meta tags, but keep in mind that they are NOT a guarantee that your site will appear first. Adding some meta tag code is not amagic bullet that cures your site of dismal rankings. For more information, see the tips on using meta tags. Site subscribers have access to extended information about meta tags.

Just Say No To Search Engine Spamming

For one thing, spamming doesn't always work with search engines. It can also backfire. Search engines may detect your spamming attempt and penalize or ban your page from their listings.

Also, search engine spamming attempts usually center around being top ranked for extremely popular keywords. You can try and fight that battle against other sites, but then be prepared to spend a lot of time each week, if not each day, defending your ranking. That effort usually would be better spent on networking and alternative forms of publicity, described below.

If those practical reasons aren't enough, how about some ethical ones? The content of most Web pages ought to be enough for search engines to determine relevancy without Webmasters having to resort to repeating keywords for no reason other than to try and "beat" other Web pages. The stakes will simply keep rising, and users will also begin to hate sites that undertake these measures.

Consider search engine spamming against spam mail. No one likes spam mail, and sites that use spam mail services often face a backlash from those on the receiving end. Sites that spam search engines degrade the value of search engine listings. As the problem grows, these sites may face the same backlash that spam mail generates.

Submit Your Key Pages

Most search engines will index the other pages from your Web site by following links from a page you submit to them. But sometimes they miss, so it's good to submit the top two or three pages that best summarize your Web site.

Don't trust the submission process to automated programs and services. Some of them are excellent, but the major search engines are too important. There aren't that many, so submit manually, so that you can see if there are any problems reported.

Also, don't bother submitting more than the top two or three pages. It doesn't speed up the process. Submitting alternative pages is only insurance. In case the search engine has trouble reaching one of the pages, you've covered yourself by giving it another page from which to begin its crawl of your site.

Some search engines have an instant indexing service, as described in the Search Engine Features page. In this cases, you should submit all the key pages from your Web site, not just the top two or three.

Be patient. It can take up to a month to two months for your "non-submitted" pages to appear in a search engine, and some search engines may not list every page from your site.

Detailed information about submitting to each major search engine is available to site subscribers.

Go to http://www.searchenginewatch.com to learn more about becoming a site subscriber

Verify And Maintain Your Listing

Check on your pages and ensure they get listed, in the ways described on the Check RL page. Once your pages are listed in a search engine, monitor your listing every week or two. Strange things happen. Pages disappear from catalogs. Links go screwy. Watch for trouble, and resubmit if you spot it.

Keep in mind that a number of the major search engines are now providing country-specific versions of their directories. These mainly work filtering sites by domain. For example, a British edition of a major search engine might only list Web sites with British domains, such as ".co.uk." A British site ending in a non-British domain, such as .com, would be filtered out. If this type of situation applies to your site, you may need to message the search engine so that they can manually include your site.

Resubmit your site any time you make significant changes. Search engines should revisit on a regular schedule. However, some search engines have grown smart enough to realize some sites only change content once or twice a year, so they may visit less often. Resubmitting after major changes will help ensure that your site's content is kept current.

Beyond Search Engines

It's worth taking the time to make your site more search engine friendly, because some simple changes may pay off with big results. Even if you don't come up in the top ten for your strategic keywords, you may find an improvement for strategic keywords you aren't anticipating. The addition of just one extra word can suddenly make a site appear more relevant, and it can be impossible to guess what that word will be.

You should also consider negotiating reciprocal links with sites that do appear in the top ten lists, if you are having no luck. Perhaps some of these sites might be considered "competitors," but you'd be surprised how many are happy to link to your site in return for a link back. After all, your site may appear first when slightly different keywords are used. Links are what the Web was built on, and they remain one of the best ways for people to find your site.

Also, remember that while search engines are a primary way people look for Web sites, but they are not the only way. People also find sites through word-of-mouth, traditional advertising, the traditional media, newsgroup postings, Web directories and links from other sites. Many times, these alternative forms are far more effective draws than are search engines. For some ideas, see some of the links on the Online Publicity page.

Finally, know when it's time to call it quits. A few changes may be enough to make you tops in one or two search engines. But that's not enough for some people, and they will invest days creating special pages and changing their sites to try and do better. This time could usually be put to better use pursuing non-search engine publicity methods.

Don't obsess over your ranking. Even if you follow every tip and find no improvement, you still have gained something. You will know that search engines are not the way you'll be attracting traffic. You can concentrate your efforts in more productive areas, rather than wasting your valuable time.

Appendix 6
How to Write and Format
a Press Release
for E-mail Distribution

This is the definitive style guide to the correct format for e-mail news releases based on feedback from journalists and reporters.

A conventional 'hard copy' press release is a brief document generally one to three double-spaced type written pages announcing news about your company, product or service to media professionals. E-mail press releases are usually shorter in length than their print counterparts. The majority of electronic news releases sent are 500 words of text organized into five, short two to three sentence paragraphs.

E-mail software allows the user to set limits on the size of messages it will download. Since many individuals do not change the default limit on their e-mail software, long messages can be truncated. For this reason we discourage clients from sending extremely lengthy electronic news releases. Information such as photographs, bios of company executives, white papers and other supporting documents usually included in a printed media kit may be published online where reporters may access them easily at their convenience.

If your company, for example, has completed an online survey of Internet shoppers, include a brief overview of the results in the electronic press release then follow that paragraph with the URL or home page address where complete survey results are published. The URLs for screen shots of your Web site and products may also be included in the news release.

Some reporters have limited online access. As a courtesy, always include a contact method for reporters who prefer to have materials mailed to them by conventional means. Sending photographs and supplemental information files through e-mail attachments is not acceptable when contacting a reporter.

Information to Include in a News Release

A compelling e-mail subject header and headline.

A first paragraph that covers the five W's: who, what, where, when and why.

Electronic contact information including an e-mail address for the press contact and Web site address of the company.

Reporters working on deadline will often choose to call a company representative rather than wait for a reply by e-mail. Be sure that in addition to e-mail contact information a phone number for the press contact is listed. The mention of key clients or endorsement from a 'non-biased' source like a university professor or a software reviewer. You should have permission from those sources to use their remarks in your press release.

A short paragraph at the end of the release containing background information about the company. This might include a synopsis of the activities of the company, how long they have been in business, and any area of expertise. If the press release is about a book or entertainer then cover career high-points.

Story Tips

Electronic PR does not differ from conventional PR in that one's ability to write and organize information well is rewarded with press coverage. However, the one-two punch of a creative subject header for your message and a clever "spin" to your news rings extra loud in a crowded inbox.

Many journalists respond to clever writing and news releases that describe how a new product or service is a solution to a business or consumer problem. Pointing to a new business, consumer or health trend is another way to position a story.

Another popular method for obtaining press coverage is to ride piggyback on a breaking news story by alerting the media to your client's expertise on that particular subject.

Like the Rolling Stones say, "Time is on your side." Be prepared to act fast if you sense a PR opportunity. Time the sending of your news release right and you can receive a windfall of publicity. That's where a service like ours can help.

In 1998, one of our software clients had the good fortune to be the only company delivering the Starr Report by e-mail using a proprietary technology for which the recipient paid to read the document. Many may remember the Starr Report was first published online. While individuals jammed Web sites attempting to read the document, our client offered the only alternative to the congestion. Following the distribution of a press release the company received thousands of requests for delivery and a once-in-a-lifetime opportunity to showcase their product.

Electronic press release delivery is an excellent tool when a story has a limited shelf-life and or when a news window will be open only for a limited time.

How to Format a Release

1. The first line of the e-mail message should read: FOR IMMEDIATE RELEASE in all caps. This lets the reporter know the news is authorized for publication on the date they receive it.

2. Allow one spacer line then write a headline using a combination of lower case and capital letters. Keep your headline to ten words or less. Do not write the headline in all capital letters because it is harder to read using e-mail software.

3. Allow another empty line for spacing, then begin the text of the release as we show with the city and state followed by a dash. All releases must include a date since reporters do not always use releases immediately.

4. There are a number of conventions for line length of electronic press releases. Xpress Press formats press release to the style most universal among e-mail readers.

5. Include press contact information below the text of the news release. A reporter reading your release should be able to make a decision about your story in the first screen of the e-mail message. Don't waste that space with contact information. They will scroll down to find out who to contact if they want to follow-up with you.

6. Finally, close the document with the characters -30- or ### which are style conventions that let the report know they have reached the end of the story.

Reminders

Don't trust your word processing program to catch errors in grammar and spelling. Have a few individuals read the release before sending it to a reporter or news agency. Although an Xpress Press staffer reads through each release, we are reading a number of stories each day looking for obvious errors like the omission of an e-mail address for the press contact.

Additionally, remember that press releases are sent by e-mail and not everyone uses the same software. For that reason we do not use HTML tags, bold type or color text which may not transmit consistently across all computer platforms.

Sample Press Releases

Below is a sample press release that generated quite a buzz for its company several years ago. Notice that the release does not follow the usual rules of including the five W's up front. However, the headline is a unique twist on words and grabs the reader's interest quickly. For more examples of successful press releases read those from Two Dog Press, Ireland's Eye and Israel Wire

FOR IMMEDIATE RELEASE

Noodle Bytes Man

DUXBURY, Mass. - April 28, 1997 (Xpress Press)- Two years ago, Raymond Lemire was at one of those proverbial crossroads in life. Having been the victim of downsizing after a corporate merger, he faced the decision of whether to continue working for someone else or to start his own business.

Armed with statistics on growing pasta consumption, articles on the explosive growth of the Internet and a second mortgage on his house, Lemire started the Flying Noodle and its Pasta of the Month Club.

His goal was to build a semi-virtual company. He would handle all the marketing, accounting and order taking from his home- based office, while the order fulfillment and warehousing would be outsourced. This would allow him to maximize time with customers and minimize his up-front capital risk and ongoing overhead expenses.

His Internet site is fast loading with whimsical noodle characters, a section on the history and lore of pasta and pasta sauces, recipes, a contest for newsletter subscribers and over 60 different pastas and 35 different pasta sauces. Customers can order via a state-of-the-art secure shopping basket system.

The Internet site opened in December 1995 to the thunderous sound of emptiness. In the world of the Internet, if you build it they will only come if you tell them you exist. Fortunately he also produced a direct mail brochure as insurance against his "sure bet" on the Internet. This bought him the necessary time to really promote the site.

Now, a year and a half later, the Flying Noodle's Internet site brings in 30% of the company's revenues. Lemire has added a Japanese language section to his Web-site and has a growing base of customers. Over 40% of the company's revenues come from repeat business and customer referrals. About 10% of his business comes from overseas customers.

His advice to anyone who is thinking of starting an online business? Don't get carried away with the hype and forget about the basics of selling. Study the direct marketing field in terms of catalog structure, language, delivery systems, guarantees and style. Make your site as interactive as possible without ignoring the most important aspect of your site - it needs to be profitable in order to survive.

And the Flying Noodle? Is it surviving? "Business is five times ahead of 1996", says Lemire. "If we continue at this pace, 1997 will be a very good year for pasta."

You can check them out at http://www.flyingnoodle.com or call for their free brochure 1-800-566-0599.

Interview Contact: Raymond K Lemire, The Big Parmesan
Telephone: 800-566-0599
bigparmesan@flyingnoodle.com
http://www.flyingnoodle.com
Flying Noodle
1 Arrowhead Road, Duxbury, Massachusetts, USA 02332
Voice 800-566-0599 (USA 011) or 781-934-1519. Fax
781-934-1527

###

When to Send Your News

Daily Newspapers

Business and general assignment reporters working for newspapers and online dailies turn around stories within 24 and 48 hours. However, feature writers are working on stories weeks in advance of publication date. Press Releases about special events or with holiday tie-ins should be sent a minimum of three weeks in advance so the reporter has ample time to research and write the story. The same is true for promoting online Webcasts and events. Three weeks is often needed to obtain coverage in Internet newsletters and online calendars.

Monthly Magazines

Monthly publications close editorial content two months in advance of the issue date. It is not unusual for writers to be deciding on story content for a December issue in September. Stories with a holiday theme should be sent to allow the reporter ample time for research and coverage.

Radio and Television

Radio or television stations may plug your Web site or product and perhaps be interested in having a representative from your company appear on one of their programs. Because interviews can be held over the telephone you might receive a call in the afternoon for a show airing that evening. Be prepared. Designate someone from your company as the spokesperson and have them prep for the show. In some cases you can ask the show's producer for a list of questions you will be asked. Plan how you will reply to the questions. Also plan how you will respond to the interviewer if they ask questions you do not wish to answer.

Copyright The Xpress Press Service 1999
http://www.xpresspress.com/PRnotes.html

Appendix 7
Microsoft's
Internet Radio Solution

Streaming radio is one of the most popular, fastest-growing areas on the Internet.

WindowsMedia.com has received as many as 2,000 requests a day from users asking to have their favorite radio station online, and more and more stations are hopping on the Internet.

Windows Media™ Technologies provide the radio-ready technology to make the transition from on the air to online both painless and economical.

Radio-Friendly Technology

With any streaming media, users don't have to download a file, they just play the audio in real time. The various components of Windows Media Technologies 4.0 provide a complete end-to-end solution for streaming radio signals to the Internet:

Windows Media Encoder provides an easy interface for encoding a radio signal and sending it over the Internet. With the release of the advanced new Windows Media Format codec, Windows Media Technologies deliver stunning audio quality over standard 28.8 kilobit per second (Kbps) Internet connections.

To play the stream, listeners use the Windows Media Player, which has been integrated into the latest release of Windows Internet Explorer as the Windows Radio toolbar. Users can even add a station to their Internet Explorer Favorites menu.

An Exploding Market for Online Radio

Research compiled by The Arbitron Company indicates that in the last quarter of 1998 and the first quarter of 1999, the percentage of Americans who listen to the radio over the Internet more than doubled. In July 1998, when the study originally took place, 6 percent of all Americans had listened to the radio over the Internet. In February 1999, numbers indicated that 13 percent of Americans had listened to the radio over the Internet.

Broadcasters have an opportunity to reach new audiences. Any station that is broadcasting online is available in the office. The vast majority of listeners to a station's Web site are in the station's metropolitan service area. Stations have the opportunity to improve ratings by increasing at-work listeners in their local areas.

What's more, this expanded listener base comes at a relatively low cost. Broadcasters can expect to pay $900 to $2,000 every month from an Internet Service Provider (ISP), depending on the amount of bandwidth their station consumes every month.

But how does a radio station make money from this new market? Right now, the Internet broadcast industry is in its infancy. Business models that test acquiring loyal customers have grown more common as the Internet distribution medium becomes a serious broadcast medium.

This is similar to the early days of Cable TV when significant new brands/value were built, as the medium grew significant. Today, advertising, e-commerce, and pay-per-view are all viable business opportunities for online broadcasters.

Support From Microsoft Programs

Programs are in place to ease the transition to online radio. The Windows Media Service Provider Program provides a list of qualified service providers who work with radio stations to stream their broadcasts. Many Internet Service Providers will gladly trade services for advertising on your station or the ability to advertise on your Web site. Microsoft also has partners that specialize in partnering with large-market radio stations to produce Web sites and to stream radio broadcasts.

See the complete listing of Windows Media service providers. These providers offer all levels of service. Once a station is broadcasting online, WindowsMedia.com provides easy access to millions of listeners. Stations streaming with Windows Media Technologies can gain instant exposure by joining the WindowsMedia.com radio program and getting a listing on the Radio Station Guide. This popular feature of WindowsMedia.com allows listeners to search for stations by both format and location and to add them to their online "radio tuner."

Start Broadcasting Now

Windows Media Technologies 4.0 and WindowsMedia.com make it so easy to enter the online market, there's no reason to wait. Simply follow the steps below:

- Contact a Windows Media service provider or an Internet Service Provider.

- Read the Taking Your Radio Station Online with Streaming Media to get your site up and streaming.

- List your station on the Windows Media Radio Station Guide. Read about Submitting your Radio Station to WindowsMedia.com, and fill out the information there. If you have date and time-specific promotions or other content that you want listed on WindowsMedia.com, send the information to wmsubmit@microsoft.com.

- reprint courtesy of Microsoft Corporation
http://www.microsoft.com

Appendix 8
Indie Music Organizations

Association for Independent Music (AFIM) - promoting the growth of the independent music business through trades shows, publications and special interest groups.
http://www.afim.org/

Secure Digital Music Initiative (SDMI) - founded to develop a specification for the secure distribution and use of music in digital form.
http://www.sdmi.org/

Kaleidospace Independent Internet Artists – promotes, distributes, and places the work by independent musicians and artists of all types.
http://www.kspace.com/

Brandnewmusic - promotes independent and unsigned musical talent.
http://www.brandnewmusic.com/

Epitonic - presenting and promoting audio offerings from independent labels and unsigned groups.
http://www.epitonic.com/

Independent Music Network (IMN TV) - broadcasting indie music clips, gigs, or sessions in different formats.
http://www.imntv.com/

POTENT-is a free online resource for talented, independent musicians to promote their work to the world.
http://www.potent.com.au/

Independent Label Resources - Large list of indie labels and resources for indie artists
http://www.musicisland.com/home.htm

TAXI - Opens doors for songwriters and musicians to get their music heard by industry pros.
http://www.taxi.com/

Appendix 9
Recording Web sites

365 Pro Audio - for the professional audio community featuring daily news updates, product reviews, and feature stories.
http://www.365proaudio.com/

Computer Music Journal
http://mitpress.mit.edu/e-journals/Computer-Music-Journal/

Digital Audio - TDK's online guide for information about CD recording via computer and stand-alone hardware, plus information about minidisks and blank CDs.
http://www.tdk.com/CDr/

EQ Magazine - presents a buyer's guide to recording and technology products. Fully searchable and updated regularly.
http://www.eqmag.com/

Mix Magazine Online - Internet edition of *Mix*, a magazine for commercial studio recording, concert sound, audio for film, and more.
http://www.mixonline.com/

ProRec - offering information resources for the recording professional with emphasis on digital audio workstations.
http://www.prorec.com/

Recording Magazine - magazine for the recording musician.
http://www.recordingmag.com/

Sound On Sound - magazine on electronic music instruments and recording equipment.
http://www.sospubs.co.uk/index.htm

Tapeless Studio, The - information and resources for computer-based multitrack recording.
http://www.tapeless.com/

Appendix 10
Online Media Sources

International Online Media Database
http://emedia1.mediainfo.com/emedia/

Newspapers Online
http://www.newspapers.com/

Internet Radio Stations Online
http://www.radiotower.com/

Online Radio Station Listings
http://www.usradio.net/

Best Online Radio Stations
http://www.startingpage.com/html/online_radio_stations.html

Indie Music Online Radio List
http://indie-music.com/radio.htm

Internet Press Release Services
http://www.newsbureau.com/

URLWire
http://www.URLwire.com/

X-Press News
http://www.xpresspress.com/

Appendix 11
Record Manufacturing
and Packaging

Creative Disk
http://www.creativedisc.com/

DiscMakers
http://www.discmakers.com/
One of the oldest and one of the best.

Oasis
http://oasisCD.com/
Oasis has created a distribution pathway (in conjunction with the largest record distributor in the world) for independent musicians' recordings to be sold at major national retail and online outlets -- an enormous leap for indies into the national scene.

Miscellaneous Resources:

New Media Digital
Webhosting and design services.
http://www.newmediadigital.com

Search Engine Watch
Everything you need to know about search engines.
http://www.searchenginewatch.com/

Anatomy of a Press Release
A quick guide to writing a press release.
http://www.pressflash.com/anatomy.html

The Music Marketing Company
Marketing, Promotion, and PR for indie musicians.
http://www.musicmarketingco.com

Software

ContactPlus
http://www.contactplus.com/
Shareware contact database software with auto-dialer.

Contact Plus – Free contact management software

AOLPress
http://www.aolpress.com
Free, excellent Web page building software with tutorials.

CuteFTP
http://www.cuteftp.com/
Great shareware utility to send your files to your server. Free trial download. Works indefinitely.

Cool Edit 2000
http://www.cooledit.com/
Will record your audio through a standard sound card in stereo.

MusicMatch Jukebox
http://www.musicmatch.com/
Converts .WAV files to MP3 files compatible with most online portal services, and is the official software for MP3.com.

Recommended Reading:

This Business of Music Marketing and Promotion by Tad Lathrop, Jim Pettigrew

Tim Sweeney's Guide to Releasing Independent Records by Tim Sweeney, Mark Geller

Guerrilla Marketing: Secrets for Making Big Profits from Your Small Business by Jay Conrad Levinson; Paperback

Survival Guide For Songwriters and Artists by Stetson G. Bailey

This Business of Artist Management by Xavier M., Jr. Frascogna, H. Lee Hetherington (Contributor)

Making and Marketing Music: The Musician's Guide to Financing, Distributing and Promoting Albums by Jodi Summers

The Billboard Guide to Music Publicity by Jim Pettigrew

This Business of Music by M. William Krasilovsky, Sidney Shemel (Contributor)

The Guerrilla Marketing Handbook by Jay Conrad Levinson, et al; Paperback

Mastering Guerrilla Marketing: 100 Profit-Producing Insights That You Can Take to the Bank by Jay Conrad Levinson; Paperback

Guerrilla Marketing Online: The Entrepreneur's Guide to Earning Profits on the Internet by Jay Conrad Levinson, Charles Rubin. Paperback

The Seven Lost Secrets of Success by Joe Vitale; Paperback

CyberWriting by Joe Vitale; Paperback

Permission Marketing: Turning Strangers Into Friends, and Friends into Customers by Seth Godin, Don Peppers (Hardcover)

Nashville's Unwritten Rules: Inside the Business of Country Music by Dan Daley (Paperback - June 1999)

Principles of Internet Marketing by Ward Hanson (Hardcover)

The Complete Guide to Publicity: Maximize Visibility for Your Product, Service, or Organization by Joe Marconi

101 Ways to Promote Yourself by Raleigh Pinskey

Six Steps to Free Publicity: And Dozens of Other Ways to Win Free Media Attention for You or Your Business by Marcia Yudkin

Public Relations on the Net: Winning Strategies to Inform and Influence the Media, the Investment Community, the Government, the Public, and More! by Shel Holtz

$10,000 of Publicity for Your Small Business by John Crane Vita

eBrands: Building an Internet Business at Breakneck Speed by Phil Carpenter

Differentiate or Die: Survival in Our Era of Killer Competition by Jack Trout, Steve Rivkin (Contributor)

The Revenge of Brand X: How to Build A Big Time Brand - on the Web or Anywhere Else by Rob Frankel

Inside the Minds: Internet Marketing - Industry Experts Reveal the Secrets to Marketing, Advertising, and Building a Successful Brand on the Internet by Ebranded Books.Com Staff

The 22 Immutable Laws of Marketing: Violate Them at Your Own Risk by Al Ries, Jack Trout

The Unabashed Self-Promoter's Guide: What Every Man, Woman, Child and Organization in America Needs to Know About Getting Ahead by Exploiting the Media by Jeffrey Lant

Start and Run Your Own Record Label by Daylle Deanna Schwartz

The Musician's Guide to Making & Selling Your Own CDs & Cassettes by Jana Stanfield

Making Money Right Now in the Music Business by Bob Baker. Paperback (June 1996)

Making Money Making Music: No Matter Where You Live by James W. Dearing.

Making Music for Money by James Lincoln, Collier.

How to Make and Sell Your Own Recording by Diane Sward Rapaport, Loreena McKennitt (Preface)

Confessions of a Record Producer by Moses Avalon

All Area Access: Personal Management for Unsigned Musicians by Marc Davison, Dan Weinstein (Illustrator)

Index

QUICK ORDER FORM

Fax Orders:
(413) 425-6421
Telephone Orders:
877-866-312-BOOK (312-2665)

E-Mail Orders:
orders@NMDBooks.Com
Website Orders:
http://www.nmdbooks.com

We accept personal checks, Visa, Mastercard and Bank Debit Cards.

To order by mail, please fill out this form and mail to:
NMD Books, Mark Curran, 2828 Cochran Street, Suite 285 Simi Valley, CA. 93065

Sell Your Music!
The Musician's Survival Guide to Direct Distribution on the Internet

# of copies	price	S&H	CA tax	Total
		Air Shipping: US $4.00 first book $2.00 each additional **Air: International** $9.00 first book $5.00 each additional	Please add 8% sales tax for products shipped to CA addresses.	
	$19.95/book			
			Total Enclosed	

Please send more FREE information on:
___Other books
___Music Marketing Services

___Speaking/Seminars
___Consulting

Name_____

Address_____

City_____State_____Zip_____-_____

Telephone_____

E-Mail Address:_____

Payment: ___Check ___Debit Card ___Master Card ___Visa

Card number:_____

Name on card:_____ Exp. date___/____

QUICK ORDER FORM

Fax Orders:
(413) 425-6421
Telephone Orders:
877-866-312-BOOK (312-2665)

E-Mail Orders:
orders@NMDBooks.Com
Website Orders:
http://www.nmdbooks.com

We accept personal checks, Visa, Mastercard and Bank Debit Cards.

To order by mail, please fill out this form and mail to:
NMD Books, Mark Curran, 2828 Cochran Street, Suite 285 Simi Valley, CA. 93065

Sell Your Music!
The Musician's Survival Guide to Direct Distribution on the Internet

# of copies	price	S&H	CA tax	Total
		Air Shipping: US $4.00 first book $2.00 each additional **Air: International** $9.00 first book $5.00 each additional	Please add 8% sales tax for products shipped to CA addresses.	
	$19.95/book			
			Total Enclosed	

Please send more FREE information on:
___Other books   ___Speaking/Seminars
___Music Marketing Services   ___Consulting

Name_____

Address_____

City_____State_____Zip_____-_____

Telephone_____

E-Mail Address:_____

Payment: ___Check ___Debit Card ___Master Card ___Visa

Card number:_____

Name on card:_____ Exp. date___/____

QUICK ORDER FORM

Fax Orders:
(413) 425-6421
Telephone Orders:
877-866-312-BOOK (312-2665)

E-Mail Orders:
orders@NMDBooks.Com
Website Orders:
http://www.nmdbooks.com

We accept personal checks, Visa, Mastercard and Bank Debit Cards.

To order by mail, please fill out this form and mail to:
NMD Books, Mark Curran, 2828 Cochran Street, Suite 285 Simi Valley, CA. 93065

Sell Your Music!
The Musician's Survival Guide to Direct Distribution on the Internet

# of copies	price	S&H	CA tax	Total
		Air Shipping: US $4.00 first book $2.00 each additional **Air: International** $9.00 first book $5.00 each additional	Please add 8% sales tax for products shipped to CA addresses.	
	$19.95/book			
			Total Enclosed	

Please send more FREE information on:
___Other books   ___Speaking/Seminars
___Music Marketing Services   ___Consulting

Name_____

Address_____

City_____State_____Zip_____-_____

Telephone_____

E-Mail Address:_____

Payment: ___Check ___Debit Card ___Master Card ___Visa

Card number:_____

Name on card:_____ Exp. date___/____

QUICK ORDER FORM

Fax Orders:
(413) 425-6421

Telephone Orders:
877-866-312-BOOK (312-2665)

E-Mail Orders:
orders@NMDBooks.Com

Website Orders:
http://www.nmdbooks.com

We accept personal checks, Visa, Mastercard and Bank Debit Cards.

To order by mail, please fill out this form and mail to:
NMD Books, Mark Curran, 2828 Cochran Street, Suite 285 Simi Valley, CA. 93065

Sell Your Music!
The Musician's Survival Guide to Direct Distribution on the Internet

# of copies	price	S&H	CA tax	Total
		Air Shipping: US $4.00 first book $2.00 each additional **Air: International** $9.00 first book $5.00 each additional	Please add 8% sales tax for products shipped to CA addresses.	
	$19.95/book			
			Total Enclosed	

Please send more FREE information on:
___Other books   ___Speaking/Seminars
___Music Marketing Services   ___Consulting

Name_____

Address_____

City_____State_____Zip_____-_____

Telephone_____

E-Mail Address:_____

Payment: ___Check ___Debit Card ___Master Card ___Visa

Card number:_____

Name on card:_____ Exp. date___/____

QUICK ORDER FORM

Fax Orders:
(413) 425-6421

Telephone Orders:
877-866-312-BOOK (312-2665)

E-Mail Orders:
orders@NMDBooks.Com

Website Orders:
http://www.nmdbooks.com

We accept personal checks, Visa, Mastercard and Bank Debit Cards.

To order by mail, please fill out this form and mail to:
NMD Books, Mark Curran, 2828 Cochran Street, Suite 285 Simi Valley, CA. 93065

Sell Your Music!
The Musician's Survival Guide to Direct Distribution on the Internet

# of copies	price	S&H	CA tax	Total
		Air Shipping: US $4.00 first book $2.00 each additional **Air: International** $9.00 first book $5.00 each additional	Please add 8% sales tax for products shipped to CA addresses.	
	$19.95/book			
			Total Enclosed	

Please send more FREE information on:
___Other books   ___Speaking/Seminars
___Music Marketing Services   ___Consulting

Name_____

Address_____

City_____State_____Zip_____-_____

Telephone_____

E-Mail Address:_____

Payment: ___Check ___Debit Card ___Master Card ___Visa

Card number:_____

Name on card:_____ Exp. date___/____